Quick Dinner Menus

FAST, FAMILY-PLEASING MEALS IN MINUTES

MARGARET HAPPEL

Butterick Publishing

The author and publisher thank the following for supplying props for use in the photography: La Cuisinière, 867 Madison Ave., New York, NY 10021; The Pottery Barn, 321 Tenth Ave., New York, NY 10011; and Villeroy and Boch, 41 Madison Ave., New York, NY 10010.

Book Design: *Betty Binns*

Photography: *Bill Helms*

Pictured on the front cover: Slavic Feast for Fall (page 102).

Library of Congress Cataloging in Publication Data

Happel, Margaret.
    Quick dinner menus.

    1. Dinners and dining.   2.   Menus.   I.   Title.
TX737.H36   641.5′55   79-9370
ISBN 0-88421-064-2

Contents

Introduction

We all enjoy a delicious, home-cooked meal, but how to prepare it when work, errands and other activities are crowding an already too-full schedule? QUICK DINNER MENUS comes to the rescue with more than 160 complete meals, each with a work plan that shows the quickest way to prepare the meal. And every dinner in this book can be made in 45 minutes or less!

Arranged by seasons, these varied, tasty meals are in sync with the weather—light spring meals, kitchen-cooling dishes for summer, heartier fare for fall and winter.

To save you even more time, here are a few hints. Try to plan a week's worth of menus and do your shopping all at once. Stock up on basics like canned and frozen fruits, vegetables, soups, meat and fish. If you have a large freezer, buying large quantities of meat on sale and freezing meal-size portions will save time later. You'll find appetizing recipes here for all sorts of convenience foods, as well as for fresh meats and produce.

Also consider investing in timesaving kitchen appliances. An electric blender, food processor and microwave oven are great helps to get you out of the kitchen fast.

Too busy to think about dinner? With QUICK DINNER MENUS you can still have a great meal—and the time to enjoy it.

Note: To let you find them easily, menus using a food processor are keyed with this symbol: .

Menus using a microwave oven are keyed with this symbol: .

Speedy Spring Suppers

Got spring fever? Planning dinner is probably the furthest thing from your mind when getting that rusty tennis game back in shape, planting the garden or throwing a bridal shower for a friend is on the agenda.

So pick a menu, any menu, from this delightful spring collection, and don't give dinner another thought. Is it still early in the season and a bit cool? Perhaps a warm Crusted Ham Baked in Beer would be just the thing, accompanied by Hot Pepper Corn Bread and Buttered Cabbage, with Lemon Walnut Parfaits for dessert.

Or if it's a warm day in May, try "Casual Dining Japanese Style": Japanese Chicken and Steak, rice and Japanese Vegetables with cool Sherbet-Filled Melon for dessert.

When friends are invited for dinner, the "Rustic French Dinner" is a perfect offering: Cornish Game Hens au Vin, new potatoes sprinkled with chopped parsley, peas and Quick Mocha Mousse. This elegant meal is so easy to prepare you'll enjoy it as much as your guests.

The recipes in this chapter—and throughout the book—creatively combine the season's fresh fruits and vegetables with timesaving convenience foods. The result in each case is the best possible meal in the shortest possible time.

With dinner plans taken care of, you can give into that spring fever.

SPECTACULAR STEAK DINNER

Porterhouse Steak with Mushroom-Walnut Sauce

Pan-Fried Potatoes
Creamed Spinach

Ice Cream Tarts

Serves 4.

1½ pints chocolate ripple ice cream

4 prepared graham cracker tart shells

one 8-ounce jar chocolate sauce

1 cup heavy cream

½ cup sliced or slivered almonds

WORK PLAN: Assemble Ice Cream Tarts (see recipe below). Peel 1 pound potatoes and cut into ¼-inch-thick slices. Fry potatoes in mixture of 2 tablespoons oil and 2 tablespoons butter or margarine; keep warm. Prepare Porterhouse Steak with Mushroom-Walnut Sauce (see recipe below). Cook two 10-ounce packages frozen-in-bag creamed spinach according to label directions.

Ice Cream Tarts

1. Divide ice cream among 4 tart shells; shape ice cream into mounds. Spoon a little chocolate sauce over each; freeze.

2. To serve, beat cream until stiff and use it to top each tart. Sprinkle each with almonds.

Porterhouse Steak with Mushroom-Walnut Sauce

2-pound porterhouse steak, 1 to 1½ inches thick

2 teaspoons salt

½ teaspoon pepper

SAUCE

2 tablespoons butter or margarine

2 cups thinly sliced mushrooms

1 tablespoon flour

1 small clove garlic, crushed

¾ cup beef broth

¼ cup dry sherry

1 tablespoon Dijon-style mustard

2 to 3 drops hot pepper sauce

¼ cup finely chopped walnuts

1. Preheat broiler.

2. Wipe steak with damp paper towels; sprinkle both sides of meat with salt and pepper. Broil 4 inches from heat, 2 minutes per side, to seal in juices; then broil 6 to 10 minutes per side.

3. To make sauce, melt butter or margarine in medium saucepan over medium heat; add mushrooms and sauté until tender, about 5 minutes, stirring constantly.

4. Add flour and garlic to mushrooms; cook 1 minute longer, stirring constantly. Reduce heat to low; blend in beef broth and sherry, stirring to keep sauce smooth.

5. Bring to boiling point, stirring constantly. Add mustard, hot pepper sauce and walnuts; heat 2 minutes longer. Serve alongside steak.

**SPRING SUPPER
JAPONAISE**

Sukiyaki

Angel Hair Noodles
Endive-Watercress Salad

Mocha Ice Cream Sundaes

Serves 4.

WORK PLAN: Prepare dessert by dividing 1 pint each chocolate and coffee ice cream among 4 individual parfait glasses, arranging in layers; sprinkle grated chocolate on top of each and freeze. To prepare salad, toss together 2 cups each bite-size pieces endive and watercress sprigs and chill; just before serving, toss with ⅓ cup oil and vinegar dressing. Prepare one 16-ounce package fine noodles according to label directions; keep warm while preparing Sukiyaki (see recipe below).

Sukiyaki

1½ pounds sirloin steak,
½ inch thick

2 tablespoons vegetable oil

2 cups thin onion rings

2 cups thinly sliced
mushrooms

one 16-ounce can bean
sprouts, rinsed and
drained

½ cup beef broth

⅓ cup dry white wine or
sherry

2 tablespoons sugar

1 tablespoon soy sauce

½ pound spinach, washed
and stems removed

1. Wipe steak well with damp paper towels. Cut meat across grain into thin strips; set aside.

2. Heat oil in large skillet, electric skillet or wok; add onions and stir-fry for 1 minute. Push onions to one side of skillet; brown beef strips quickly, about 1 minute per side.

3. Stir in mushrooms; stir-fry 1 minute longer. Add bean sprouts, beef broth, white wine or sherry, sugar and soy sauce. Bring to simmering point, stirring constantly. Add spinach leaves; stir until spinach is slightly wilted.

**EASY
STIR-FRY
SUPPER**

Egg Drop Soup

Beef and Bean Sprouts

Rice
Stir-Fried Carrots

Orange Sherbet

Serves 4.

WORK PLAN: Prepare dessert: Divide 1½ pints orange sherbet among 4 dessert glasses; top each with a little grated orange rind and freeze. Cook 1 cup long-grain rice according to label directions; keep warm. To prepare soup, heat two 10½-ounce cans beef broth to simmering point; pour 1 beaten egg through fine sieve into broth to form "noodles"; keep warm. Peel 1 pound carrots; using vegetable parer, slice diagonally into paper-thin circles. Heat 2 tablespoons oil in large skillet; add carrots and stir-fry until crisp-tender, about 3 minutes. Sprinkle with 1 teaspoon salt and ¼ teaspoon pepper. At the same time, prepare Beef and Bean Sprouts (see recipe below).

Beef and Bean Sprouts

½ pound flank steak

2 tablespoons vegetable oil

one 16-ounce can bean sprouts, rinsed and drained

2 tablespoons dry sherry

1 tablespoon soy sauce

1 tablespoon cornstarch

1 tablespoon water

1. Wipe steak well with damp paper towels; cut steak crosswise against the grain into paper-thin strips (this is best done if the meat is slightly frozen). Set meat aside.

2. Heat oil in large skillet, electric skillet or wok; add beef and stir-fry for about 30 seconds, separating pieces constantly.

3. Add bean sprouts; cook for 30 seconds, stirring constantly. Add sherry and soy sauce; cook 30 seconds longer, stirring constantly.

4. Blend cornstarch with water and add to beef mixture; cook for 1 minute or until mixture thickens, stirring constantly.

QUICK COMPANY MENU

Chilly Pea Soup

Skillet Spanish Beef

Herb and Wild Rice

Cabbage-Carrot Slaw

Apricots with Ginger Topping

Serves 4.

WORK PLAN: To prepare soup, blend one 11¼-ounce can green pea soup with ½ cup sour cream and ½ cup dry sherry. Sprinkle with ¼ cup snipped fresh or frozen chives; chill. Next, prepare Cabbage-Carrot Slaw (see recipe below). Prepare dessert: Divide one 20-ounce can apricot halves among 4 dessert glasses; top with one 3¾-ounce package instant vanilla pudding and pie filling made according to label directions, stirring in ¼ cup chopped crystallized ginger. Prepare one 6-ounce package herb and wild rice mix according to label directions. Meanwhile, prepare Skillet Spanish Beef (see recipe below).

Cabbage-Carrot Slaw

half of small head cabbage, cut into thin wedges

2 medium carrots, peeled and cut into 3-inch pieces

1 medium onion, peeled and quartered

½ cup mayonnaise

½ cup sour cream

2 teaspoons grated lemon rind

2 teaspoons celery seed

1 teaspoon salt

¼ teaspoon pepper

1. With steel slicing blade in place in food processor, place cabbage wedges one at a time in tube in processor lid. Slice by pressing down pusher. Repeat to shred all cabbage. Shred carrots and onion the same way.

2. Place shredded vegetables in large bowl. Stir in mayonnaise, sour cream, lemon rind, celery seed, salt and pepper. Chill slaw until serving time.

Skillet Spanish Beef

1 pound boneless lean beef, cut into 1-inch cubes

2 stalks celery, cut into 2-inch pieces

1 large onion, peeled and quartered

2 tablespoons butter or margarine

1 teaspoon salt

¼ teaspoon pepper

one 8-ounce can Spanish-style tomato sauce

½ cup sliced stuffed olives

1. With steel all-purpose blade in place in food processor, place half of beef in processor bowl. Chop finely by turning machine on and off for about 5 seconds. Place in mixing bowl. Repeat to chop remaining meat.

2. Place celery and onion in processor bowl; chop finely by turning machine on and off for about 10 seconds. Melt butter or margarine in large skillet over medium heat; add beef, celery and onion and sauté for 5 minutes, stirring constantly.

3. Add salt, pepper and tomato sauce. Reduce heat to low and cook, covered, for 15 minutes. Place in heated serving bowl; sprinkle with sliced olives.

LITTLE LEAGUE SPECIAL

Potato-Chive Soup

Inside-Out Burgers

Strawberry Ice Cream
Pecan Cookies
Serves 4.

WORK PLAN: Divide 1½ pints strawberry ice cream among 4 individual dessert dishes; freeze. Serve for dessert with store-bought pecan cookies. Prepare Inside-Out Burgers (see recipe below). Prepare one 10¾-ounce can potato soup according to label directions, stirring in 2 tablespoons snipped fresh or frozen chives.

Inside-Out Burgers

1½ pounds ground beef

4 thin slices onion

4 thin slices tomato

4 thin slices sharp Cheddar cheese, or 4 slices American cheese

4 slices pickle

2 tablespoons butter or margarine

2 teaspoons salt

½ teaspoon pepper

4 hamburger buns

1. Divide beef into 8 equal parts; flatten each portion into 4-inch rounds. On 4 rounds, place 1 onion slice, 1 tomato slice, 1 cheese slice and 1 pickle slice. Cover each portion with a second beef round. Seal edges by pressing tightly.

2. Melt butter or margarine in large heavy skillet over medium heat; add burgers and brown, 3 to 7 minutes per side, sprinkling each cooked side with some salt and pepper.

3. Split and toast hamburger buns; serve each hamburger between bun halves.

**RAINY DAY
DINNER**

Broiled Grapefruit

**Roast Beef Hash Swedish
Style**

Brussels Sprouts

Mocha Cinnamon Ice Cream
Balls
Serves 4.

WORK PLAN: First prepare dessert: Scoop 1½ pints vanilla ice cream into 4 large balls; set in freezer on cookie sheet. Mix ½ cup sweetened chocolate powder, 2 teaspoons instant coffee and 1 teaspoon cinnamon; sprinkle over balls through fine sieve and return ice cream to freezer. Serve in bowls with one-fourth of one 4-ounce jar chocolate sauce over each. Prepare Roast Beef Hash Swedish Style (see recipe below). While hash is cooking, prepare two 10-ounce packages frozen Brussels sprouts according to label directions; keep warm. Prepare 4 grapefruit halves by cutting and loosening segments, sprinkling each with 2 tablespoons brown sugar and broiling 6 inches from heat for 5 minutes.

Roast Beef Hash Swedish Style

2 **medium potatoes, peeled
and quartered**

1 **medium onion, peeled
and quartered**

1 **pound cooked roast beef,
cut into 1-inch cubes**

1 **tablespoon soy sauce**

¼ **teaspoon pepper**

½ **cup butter or margarine**

4 **eggs**

1. With steel shredding blade in place in food processor, place potato quarters cut side down in tube in processor lid. Shred potatoes by pressing down pusher; place in mixing bowl.

2. With steel cutting blade in place in food processor, place onion, beef, soy sauce and pepper in food processor bowl. Chop coarsely by turning machine on and off for 10 to 15 seconds.

3. Add beef mixture to shredded potato; mix well. Melt ¼ cup of the butter or margarine in large skillet over medium heat; add hash and cook for about 15 minutes, until crust forms on bottom.

4. Invert hash onto platter and slip back into skillet to brown other side, cooking for about 10 minutes. Place on serving platter; keep hash warm.

5. Fry eggs in remaining ¼ cup butter or margarine. Serve fried eggs alongside hash.

TimeSaving Tip: The food processor is *the* timesaving machine. Preparation of food that once took several minutes now takes only seconds; for example, switching the processor on and off rapidly for a 10- to 15-second period will shred about a pound of potatoes. Always remember how fast the food processor works, and take care not to overprocess.

CALIFORNIA CHILI SUPPER

Avocado-Grapefruit Salad

Microwave Chili

Hot Corn Toaster Muffins

Caramel Custard

Serves 4.

WORK PLAN: Start by preparing Caramel Custard (see recipe below). Then prepare salad: Arrange 2 sliced avocados and segments from 2 yellow grapefruit on 4 lettuce-lined salad platters; spoon 2 tablespoons Italian-style salad dressing over each salad and chill. Prepare Microwave Chili (see recipe below). While chili is standing at room temperature, place 4 corn toaster muffins in large plastic bag; microwave on high setting for 2 minutes to warm.

Caramel Custard

⅔ cup sugar

1 tablespoon water

1¼ cups milk

4 eggs

1 tablespoon rum, or 1 teaspoon rum extract

¼ teaspoon nutmeg

1. Combine ⅓ cup of the sugar and the water in 1-quart glass casserole. Microwave on high setting for 2 minutes; stir and microwave on high setting 3 minutes longer. Pour caramel into four 6-ounce glass custard cups.

2. Pour milk into 4-cup glass measure; microwave on high setting for 2 minutes to heat milk. In small bowl, beat together eggs, remaining ⅓ cup sugar, the rum or rum extract and nutmeg.

3. Pour egg mixture into hot milk, beating constantly. Divide mixture among the custard cups. Microwave on high setting for 4 to 4½ minutes or until just set. Turn cups a quarter turn every minute to cook evenly. Cool and chill. To serve, invert onto individual dessert plates if desired.

Microwave Chili

1 pound ground beef

1 cup chopped green pepper

one 1¾-ounce package chili seasoning mix

one 20-ounce can red kidney beans

one 16-ounce can stewed tomatoes

1. Combine ground beef and green pepper in 2-quart glass casserole. Cover dish tightly with plastic wrap; microwave on high setting for 2 minutes.

2. Stir to break meat into small pieces; re-cover and microwave on high setting 2 minutes longer. Drain fat from casserole and stir to break up meat.

3. Blend in seasoning mix, undrained beans and stewed tomatoes. Stir to break up tomatoes and blend ingredients.

4. Re-cover dish and microwave on high setting for 8 minutes or on 80% power for 10 minutes. Stir chili and re-cover, rotating dish halfway through cooking process. Let stand, covered, at room temperature for 2 minutes before serving.

MENU FOR
A BUSY DAY

**Skillet Meat Loaves with
Mushroom Gravy**

Herbed Rice
Broccoli Almondine

Banana-Peach Pie

Serves 4.

WORK PLAN: Prepare Skillet Meat Loaves with Mushroom Gravy (see recipe below). Prepare dessert by placing 2 thinly sliced bananas in bottom of one 8-inch prepared graham cracker pie shell. Top with one 21-ounce can peach pie filling and decorate with refrigerator dessert topping; chill. Prepare one 16-ounce polybag frozen broccoli spears according to label directions; toss with 2 tablespoons butter or margarine and sprinkle with ¼ cup slivered almonds. Prepare one 6-ounce package herbed rice mix according to label directions.

Skillet Meat Loaves with
Mushroom Gravy

1½ pounds ground beef

**¾ cup quick-cooking
oatmeal**

**¼ cup finely chopped green
pepper**

**1 tablespoon instant minced
onion**

1 teaspoon salt

¼ teaspoon pepper

1 egg, beaten

**2 tablespoons butter or
margarine**

**one 10¾-ounce can golden
mushroom soup**

½ cup dry red wine

1. In large bowl, combine ground beef, oatmeal, green pepper, minced onion, salt, pepper and beaten egg; mix well. Shape into 4 oval-shaped meat loaves 1½ inches thick.

2. Melt butter or margarine in large skillet over medium heat; add meat loaves and brown, 2 minutes per side. Drain surplus fat from skillet.

3. Combine mushroom soup and wine; pour around meat loaves. Reduce heat to low and simmer, covered, for 20 to 25 minutes, or until meat loaves are cooked through.

WARM-WEATHER
CURRY DINNER

Hamburger Curry

Hot Rice
Cucumbers with Yogurt

Heavenly Fruit

Serves 4.

WORK PLAN: Remove one 16-ounce container frozen mixed fruits from freezer to thaw. Prepare Hamburger Curry (see recipe below). Peel and seed 4 medium cucumbers, cut into julienne strips and toss with 1 cup unflavored yogurt and 2 teaspoons grated lemon rind; chill. To make dessert, divide mixed fruit among 4 dessert glasses, sprinkle with white rum or orange juice, top with refrigerator dessert topping and sprinkle with coconut. Prepare quick-cooking rice for 4 servings according to label directions, adding 2 teaspoons paprika and 3 to 4 drops hot pepper sauce to cooking liquid.

Hamburger Curry

1 **pound ground beef**
¼ **cup chopped onion**
1½ **teaspoons curry powder**
3 **tablespoons flour**
½ **teaspoon salt**
½ **teaspoon cinnamon**
⅛ **teaspoon ginger**
1 **cup beef broth**
1 **cup milk**
1 **tablespoon lemon juice**

1. Brown ground beef in medium saucepan over medium heat for 4 to 5 minutes, stirring to break meat into small pieces. Remove from skillet with slotted spoon and set aside.

2. Pour all but 2 tablespoons drippings from skillet. Add onion and curry to drippings in skillet and sauté until onion is soft but not brown, about 3 minutes. Blend in flour, salt, cinnamon and ginger; cook until mixture is smooth and bubbly, stirring constantly.

3. Remove from heat. Slowly stir in beef broth; blend until smooth. Add milk and return to heat. Bring to boiling point, stirring constantly; cook for 1 minute. Add drained beef; reduce heat and simmer for 5 minutes, stirring occasionally. Stir in lemon juice.

**FAST
ORIENTAL
EATING**

Sweet and Pungent Beef

Hot Crisp Noodles
Chinese-Style Vegetables

Lime Sherbet
Almond Cookies
Serves 4.

1 **pound ground beef**
one 8-ounce can pineapple chunks
1 **cup beef broth**
2 **tablespoons vinegar**
2 **tablespoons soy sauce**
¼ **cup brown sugar**
2 **tablespoons cornstarch**
¼ **teaspoon dry mustard**
⅛ **teaspoon garlic powder**
⅛ **teaspoon ginger**
2 **to 4 tablespoons dry sherry**

WORK PLAN: Divide 1½ pints lime sherbet among 4 dessert dishes. Set in freezer until dessert time; serve with store-bought almond cookies. Place crisp Chinese noodles from two 3½-ounce cans in covered casserole in 300° F oven to warm while making Sweet and Pungent Beef (see recipe below). Prepare two 10-ounce packages Chinese-style vegetables according to label directions.

Sweet and Pungent Beef

1. Brown ground beef in medium skillet over medium heat for 4 to 5 minutes. Remove from skillet with slotted spoon and set aside.

2. Drain juice from pineapple chunks into large liquid measure and set pineapple aside. Add beef broth, vinegar and soy sauce to juice.

3. Blend brown sugar, cornstarch, dry mustard, garlic powder and ginger into drippings in skillet. Gradually stir in pineapple juice mixture. Bring to boiling point over medium heat, stirring until sauce is thick and translucent.

4. Stir in sherry to taste along with browned beef and drained pineapple chunks. Reduce heat to low and simmer for 4 to 5 minutes, stirring occasionally.

SOUTH-OF-THE-BORDER PATIO SUPPER

Mexican Tacos

Hot Corn Bread

Pears in Chocolate Sauce
Serves 4.

WORK PLAN: Prepare dessert: Drain one 16-ounce can pear halves and place 1 or 2 pear halves in each of 4 dessert dishes; chill. Blend two 5-ounce individual-size cans chocolate pudding with ¼ cup heavy cream and ½ teaspoon cinnamon; chill. Pour sauce over pears just before serving. Prepare one 10-ounce package corn bread mix according to label directions. While it bakes, make Mexican Tacos (see recipe below).

Mexican Tacos

1 pound ground beef

one 8-ounce can tomato sauce

1 tablespoon instant minced onion

½ teaspoon salt

½ teaspoon oregano

½ teaspoon garlic powder

¼ teaspoon pepper

¼ teaspoon cumin

one 5-ounce package precooked taco shells

TOPPINGS

2 cups shredded lettuce

2 tomatoes, sliced

1 avocado, cut into chunks

1 cup sour cream

1 cup shredded mozzarella cheese

1. Slowly brown ground beef in large skillet over low heat for 3 to 4 minutes, stirring constantly. Drain surplus fat from skillet.

2. Stir ½ cup of the tomato sauce, the minced onion, salt, oregano, garlic powder, pepper and cumin into beef in skillet. Simmer, covered, for 10 minutes, stirring occasionally.

3. While beef is cooking, heat taco shells in 350° F oven for 10 minutes. Place toppings in individual dishes. Blend remaining ½ cup tomato sauce into hot pepper sauce.

4. Fill taco shells with 3 to 4 tablespoons meat mixture. Serve toppings alongside.

JOGGERS' CASSEROLE SUPPER

Ziti Casserole

Watercress and Chicory Salad

Fruit Cocktail with Vanilla Sauce
Serves 4.

WORK PLAN: Prepare Ziti Casserole (see recipe below). Prepare salad by tossing together 2 cups watercress sprigs and 2 cups bite-size pieces chicory; chill, and toss with oil and vinegar just before serving. Divide one 16-ounce can fruit cocktail among 4 dessert dishes and chill; serve topped with sauce made by blending two 5-ounce individual-size cans vanilla pudding, ¼ cup heavy cream and ½ teaspoon grated lemon rind.

Ziti Casserole

one 8-ounce box ziti or
 rigatoni

½ pound ground beef

1 cup small curd cottage
 cheese

one 8-ounce package
 shredded mozzarella
 cheese

½ cup grated Parmesan
 cheese

one 15-ounce jar marinara
 sauce

1. Cook pasta according to label directions; drain.

2. Meanwhile, slowly brown ground beef in large skillet over low
heat for 3 to 4 minutes, stirring constantly to break meat into small
pieces. Drain surplus fat from skillet.

3. Remove skillet from heat; stir in cottage cheese, half of mozzarella cheese and half of Parmesan cheese. Add drained pasta; stir to
mix well.

4. Pour half of marinara sauce into lightly greased 2½-quart casserole; add pasta-meat mixture. Top with remaining marinara sauce;
sprinkle with remaining mozzarella and Parmesan cheese. Bake at
425° F for 25 minutes or until casserole bubbles and is very hot.

**DINNER
PRIMAVERA**

Veal and Peppers

Linguine

Green Salad with Italian
Dressing

Pudding Inglese

Serves 4.

WORK PLAN: Prepare Pudding Inglese, then Veal and Peppers (see
recipes below). Cook one 8-ounce package linguine according to
label directions. To prepare salad, combine 2 cups each bite-size
pieces romaine and escarole lettuce; toss with ⅓ cup Italian-style
dressing just before serving.

Pudding Inglese

one 3¾-ounce package
 vanilla pudding and pie
 filling

2 cups milk

¼ cup finely chopped
 mixed candied fruits

1 tablespoon grated orange
 rind

1. In 4-cup glass measure, blend vanilla pudding and pie filling and
milk; mix very well. Microwave on high setting for 6 minutes. Stir
twice during last 2 minutes of cooking time.

2. Remove from microwave oven; stir in candied fruits and orange
rind. Pour into 4 individual serving dishes.

Veal and Peppers

1½ pounds boneless veal
  shoulder, cut into ¾-inch
  cubes

2 tablespoons olive oil

one 15-ounce jar marinara
  sauce

¼ cup chopped parsley

1 envelope beef powder
  concentrate

½ teaspoon salt

¼ teaspoon pepper

¼ teaspoon thyme

2 to 3 drops hot pepper sauce

2 cups green pepper strips

1. Toss together veal and oil in 2-quart glass casserole. Cover dish tightly with glass lid or plastic wrap; microwave on high setting for 2 minutes.

2. Add marinara sauce, parsley, beef concentrate, salt, pepper, thyme and hot pepper sauce. Cover casserole and microwave on 50% power for 14 minutes.

3. Add green pepper strips; microwave on 50% power 14 minutes longer. Let casserole stand, covered, at room temperature for 5 minutes before serving.

ELEGANT
SPRING MEAL

Celery, Fennel and Onion
Salad

Veal Chops Provençal

Rice
Peas and Mushrooms

Pears Flambé

Serves 4.

WORK PLAN: Prepare salad by combining 1½ cups each thinly sliced celery and fennel with 1 cup thin onion rings. Place mixture on 4 lettuce-lined salad plates and top with dressing made of ½ cup each sour cream and mayonnaise and 2 teaspoons grated lemon rind; chill. To prepare dessert, drain one 20-ounce can pear halves; place pears in lightly greased 8 x 8 x 2-inch baking dish and brush with ½ cup apricot preserves. Just before serving, warm ½ cup rum in small skillet over low heat; ignite, and pour flaming rum over pears. Prepare Veal Chops Provençal (see recipe below) and cook 1 cup long-grain rice according to label directions. Prepare one 16-ounce polybag frozen peas and mushrooms according to label directions.

Veal Chops Provençal

4 veal shoulder chops,
  about ¾ inch thick

¼ cup flour

¼ cup butter or margarine

½ cup chopped onion

one 8-ounce can stewed
  tomatoes

¼ cup chopped parsley

1 teaspoon marjoram

½ teaspoon salt

¼ teaspoon pepper

1. Wipe veal chops with damp paper towels; sprinkle both sides of each chop with flour, rubbing well into surfaces.

2. Melt butter or margarine in large skillet over medium heat; add chops and sauté to brown, about 2 minutes per side. Remove from skillet and set aside.

3. Add onion to drippings in skillet and sauté until tender, about 2 minutes. Reduce heat to low and add stewed tomatoes, parsley, marjoram, salt and pepper; stir to mix well. Return veal chops to skillet; simmer, covered, for 20 minutes or until chops are tender.

Celery Soup

**Pork, Rice and Tomato
Casserole**

Broccoli Hollandaise

Raspberry Trifles

Serves 4.

WORK PLAN: To prepare dessert, cut eight ¼-inch-thick slices from store-bought pound cake; sandwich slices together with raspberry preserves. Cut into ¼-inch cubes and divide among 4 dessert dishes. Divide one 12-ounce package frozen raspberries, thawed, among the dessert dishes; top with vanilla pudding from four 5-ounce individual-size cans and a swirl of whipped cream. Prepare Pork, Rice and Tomato Casserole (see recipe below). Cook two 10-ounce packages frozen broccoli spears according to label directions. Make sauce for broccoli by heating mixture of ½ cup each sour cream and mayonnaise, 2 tablespoons lemon juice and 1 teaspoon grated lemon rind. Prepare soup by heating two 10¾-ounce cans chicken broth with ¾ cup paper-thin slices celery.

Pork, Rice and Tomato Casserole

**4 pork loin chops, ¾ to 1
inch thick**

**2 tablespoons butter or
margarine**

**1 cup uncooked long-grain
rice**

1 teaspoon salt

¼ teaspoon pepper

**one 14½-ounce can stewed
tomatoes**

1½ cups dry white wine

4 thick slices onion

1. Wipe pork chops with damp paper towels. Melt butter or margarine in large skillet over medium heat; add chops and sauté to brown, about 2 minutes per side. Remove from skillet and set aside.

2. Add rice to drippings in skillet and sauté for about 2 minutes, until golden; stir in salt and pepper. Add stewed tomatoes and wine; bring to boiling point.

3. Reduce heat to low; return pork chops to skillet. Top each with onion slice. Simmer, covered, over low heat until rice is tender, about 20 to 25 minutes, adding more liquid if necessary.

Lemon Soup

Sweet-Sour Pork

Stir-Fried Cabbage

Ginger Melon

Serves 4.

WORK PLAN: Start by preparing soup: Heat two 10¾-ounce cans chicken broth with 2 tablespoons each lemon juice and chopped parsley; keep warm. Then prepare dessert: Remove seeds from one small honeydew melon; cut fruit into bite-size chunks and place in large dessert bowl. Toss with ½ cup chopped crystallized ginger; chill until serving time. Prepare Sweet-Sour Pork (see recipe below). At the same time, heat 1 tablespoon oil in large skillet; add 4 cups shredded Chinese cabbage, 1 teaspoon salt and ¼ teaspoon pepper and stir-fry until cabbage is crisp-tender.

Sweet-Sour Pork

2 tablespoons vegetable oil

2 cups finely diced cooked pork

4 green onions, cut into 1-inch pieces

1 clove garlic, crushed

one 10-ounce package frozen Hawaiian-style vegetables

one 8-ounce can pineapple chunks

2 tablespoons brown sugar

1 tablespoon cornstarch

¼ teaspoon ginger

2 tablespoons vinegar

1. Heat oil in large skillet, electric skillet or wok; add pork, green onions and garlic and stir-fry for 3 minutes.

2. Add frozen vegetables; stir-fry for 2 to 3 minutes to break up into small pieces. Drain pineapple, reserving juice; add pineapple chunks to pork mixture and stir-fry 1 minute longer.

3. In small bowl, blend brown sugar, cornstarch and ginger with reserved pineapple juice. Pour over pork and vegetable mixture; stir and cook for 1 to 2 minutes, until sauce comes to boiling point. Stir in vinegar; cook 30 seconds longer.

NOTE: This is an ideal use for leftover pork.

**AMERICAN
COUNTRY
SUPPER**

Chilled Tomato Juice

Crusted Ham Baked in Beer

Hot Pepper Corn Bread
Buttered Cabbage

Lemon Walnut Parfaits
Serves 4.

WORK PLAN: Divide 3 cups spicy tomato juice among 4 serving glasses; chill. Prepare Crusted Ham Baked in Beer (see recipe below). Prepare one 10-ounce package corn bread mix according to label directions, adding 1 teaspoon coarsely crushed black pepper. Prepare dessert: Grind ½ cup walnuts in blender or food processor; prepare one 3¾-ounce package instant lemon pudding according to label directions. Fold walnuts into pudding and divide among 4 parfait glasses; chill. Cook 4 cups finely shredded cabbage in ½ cup boiling salted water until crisp-tender; drain. Add 2 tablespoons butter or margarine and ¼ teaspoon each pepper and nutmeg.

Crusted Ham Baked in Beer

1½-pound canned ham

one 8-ounce can crushed pineapple

¼ cup brown sugar, firmly packed

¼ teaspoon dry mustard

⅛ teaspoon ground cloves

½ cup beer or ginger ale

1. Preheat oven to 425° F. Place ham in lightly greased 1-quart baking dish.

2. In small bowl, blend 1 tablespoon pineapple juice from crushed pineapple, the brown sugar, dry mustard and cloves. Spread half of mixture over top of ham. Pour beer or ginger ale around ham.

3. Reduce oven heat to 350° F. Bake ham for 10 minutes; spread remaining sugar mixture over ham and bake 15 minutes longer. Completely drain crushed pineapple and place on top of ham; bake 10 minutes longer.

**HEARTY
HURRY-UP DINNER**

Black Bean Soup

**Ham Patties with Pineapple
Rings**

Mashed Potatoes

Mocha Bit Brownies

Serves 4.

WORK PLAN: Prepare Mocha Bit Brownies (see recipe below). Heat one 11-ounce can black bean soup according to label directions; keep warm. Just before serving soup, stir in 2 tablespoons each lemon juice and chopped parsley. Prepare Ham Patties with Pineapple Rings (see recipe below). Meanwhile, prepare instant mashed potatoes to yield 4 servings.

Mocha Bit Brownies

1 cup sugar

two 1-ounce squares
  unsweetened chocolate

1 teaspoon instant coffee

½ cup butter or margarine

2 eggs

1 teaspoon vanilla extract

¾ cup flour

½ teaspoon baking powder

one 6-ounce package
  semisweet chocolate
  morsels

Makes 16 brownies.

1. Preheat oven to 350° F.

2. In small heavy saucepan, combine sugar, chocolate and instant coffee. Melt over low heat, stirring constantly with wooden spoon.

3. With plastic blade in place in food processor, place butter or margarine in food processor bowl. Process for 10 to 15 seconds.

4. Add chocolate mixture to butter or margarine; process until well blended, about 3 seconds. Add eggs, vanilla extract, flour and baking powder; process for 10 seconds to blend.

5. Add chocolate morsels; process for 1 second. Spread batter in lightly greased 8 x 8 x 2-inch baking pan; bake for 30 minutes. Cool in pan on wire rack for 10 to 15 minutes; cut into 2-inch squares.

Ham Patties with Pineapple Rings

1½ pounds precooked ham,
  cut into 1-inch cubes

2 slices bread, quartered

1 medium onion, peeled
  and quartered

¼ cup parsley sprigs

2 eggs

2 tablespoons chili sauce or
  ketchup

1 tablespoon prepared spicy
  mustard

2 tablespoons butter or
  margarine

one 16-ounce can pineapple
  rings, drained

1. With steel cutting blade in place in food processor, place ham in food processor bowl. Finely chop ham by rapidly turning machine on and off for 10 to 15 seconds. Place ham in mixing bowl.

2. Place bread and onion in food processor bowl; chop by turning machine on and off for 10 seconds. Return ham to food processor bowl; add parsley, eggs, chili sauce or ketchup, and mustard. Process until just mixed, turning machine on and off twice for about 5 seconds each time. Shape mixture into 4 patties.

3. Melt butter or margarine in large skillet over medium heat; add patties and sauté on both sides until brown, about 10 minutes. Remove from skillet to serving platter; keep warm.

4. Add pineapple rings to drippings in skillet and sauté until brown and hot. Serve on platter with ham patties.

ITALIAN SPRINGFEST

Minestrone

Spaghetti with Tomato Meat Sauce

Mixed Green Salad with Garlic Dressing

Orange-Pineapple Ice

Serves 4.

WORK PLAN: To prepare salad, chill 6 cups bite-size pieces mixed salad greens (watercress, romaine lettuce and spinach); toss with ½ cup garlic-flavored salad dressing just before serving. Heat one 10½-ounce can minestrone with ¾ cup water and ¼ cup dry sherry; keep warm. Just before serving, sprinkle with ¼ cup chopped parsley. Prepare Spaghetti with Tomato Meat Sauce (see recipe below). At dessert time, finish preparing Orange-Pineapple Ice (see recipe below).

NOTE: Orange-Pineapple Ice must be blended and frozen overnight or made first thing in the morning. Final preparation is done just before serving.

Spaghetti with Tomato Meat Sauce

½ **pound Italian-style sausages**

1 **medium onion, peeled and quartered**

2 **cloves garlic, peeled**

¼ **cup olive or vegetable oil**

one 35-ounce can Italian-style tomatoes with basil

2 **teaspoons basil**

1 **teaspoon salt**

¼ **teaspoon pepper**

¼ **cup grated Parmesan cheese**

one 16-ounce package spaghetti

1. Remove meat from sausage casings and crumble meat into large skillet. Sauté over medium heat for about 5 minutes, stirring to break meat into small pieces. Remove from skillet with slotted spoon and set aside. Pour drippings from skillet and wipe skillet clean.

2. With steel blade in place in food processor, place onion and garlic in tube in processor lid; push through to slice.

3. Heat oil in same skillet over medium heat; add onion and garlic and sauté until golden, about 5 minutes, stirring occasionally. Drain tomato liquid into skillet.

4. With steel all-purpose blade in place in food processor, place drained tomatoes in processor bowl. Process 5 seconds to chop. Add to skillet along with basil, salt and pepper.

5. Reduce heat to low; add sausage and grated cheese. Simmer, covered, for 20 minutes.

6. Meanwhile, cook spaghetti according to label directions. Drain; place in large heated serving bowl and toss with sauce.

Orange-Pineapple Ice

one 20-ounce can crushed
  pineapple in natural juices
one 6-ounce can frozen
  orange juice concentrate
1 cup water
¼ cup sugar

1. With steel all-purpose blade in place in food processor, place undrained crushed pineapple, frozen orange juice concentrate, water and sugar in food processor bowl. Process until smooth and well blended. Pour into ice cube tray (with dividers) and freeze for 4 hours or overnight.

2. Just before serving, set steel all-purpose blade in place; place half of frozen cubes in bowl of food processor. Process until ice is finely chopped, turning machine on and off rapidly for 2 minutes. Repeat with remaining ice cubes.

**EASY
BACKYARD DINING**

Vegetable Relishes
Cheese Dip

Corn Bread and Frank Bake

Glazed Onions

Chocolate Ripple

Serves 4.

WORK PLAN: Make dip by blending ¾ cup each mayonnaise and sour cream with one 3-ounce package blue cheese, crumbled. Prepare relishes by cutting 4 stalks celery and 4 peeled carrots into strips; wash 1 package fresh radishes, trimming off root ends. Chill vegetables and dip. Prepare Corn Bread and Frank Bake (see recipe below). Meanwhile, heat ¼ cup butter or margarine and ¼ cup brown sugar, firmly packed, in large skillet. Add two 15-ounce cans whole onions, drained; heat and stir until onions are glazed. Prepare dessert by whipping 1 cup heavy cream until stiff, beating in 2 tablespoons sugar; fold in one 5-ounce individual-size can chocolate pudding, divide among 4 parfait glasses and chill.

Corn Bread and Frank Bake

1 cup yellow cornmeal
1 cup all-purpose flour
¼ cup sugar
1 tablespoon baking
  powder
1 teaspoon salt
1 cup milk
¼ cup vegetable oil
1 egg
one 6-ounce can Mexican-
  style corn, drained
1 pound frankfurters

1. Preheat oven to 425° F.

2. In large bowl, combine cornmeal, flour, sugar, baking powder and salt. Beat together milk, oil and egg; stir into cornmeal mixture just until dry ingredients are moistened. Fold in drained corn.

3. Spread mixture evenly in lightly greased 8 x 8 x 2-inch baking dish. Arrange frankfurters in two parallel lines on top of batter. Bake for 25 minutes.

FAST AND FILLING
SUPPER

Chilly Tomato Juice Cocktail

**Smoky Frankfurter and
Grits Casserole**

Okra
Cole Slaw

Ambrosia

Serves 4.

WORK PLAN: Prepare Smoky Frankfurter and Grits Casserole (see recipe below). Make dessert by dividing one 16-ounce can pineapple chunks and one 11-ounce can mandarin orange slices among 4 dessert glasses; sprinkle with coconut and chill. For appetizer, spice 3 cups bottled tomato juice with Worcestershire sauce, celery salt and hot pepper sauce to taste; pour into four 8-ounce glasses, garnish with lemon wedges and chill. Place one 16-ounce container store-bought cole slaw in lettuce-lined bowl; chill. Cook two 10-ounce packages frozen sliced okra according to label directions; drain, and serve with main course.

Smoky Frankfurter and Grits Casserole

3 cups water

¾ cup quick-cooking grits

¾ teaspoon salt

1 cup grated sharp Cheddar cheese

¼ cup butter or margarine

1 tablespoon instant minced onion

¼ teaspoon pepper

1 pound smoke-flavored frankfurters

1. Bring water to boiling point in medium saucepan over medium heat; slowly stir in grits and add salt. Bring to boiling point, stirring constantly; reduce heat to low and simmer for 4 minutes, stirring to prevent sticking.

2. Remove from heat; beat in grated cheese, butter or margarine, minced onion and pepper. Pour into well-greased 1½-quart casserole. Arrange frankfurters on top of grits in spoke design. Bake at 450° F for 20 to 30 minutes or until frankfurters are browned and grits have golden crust.

MEAL FOR
A LATE FROST

Knockwurst and Winekraut

Spicy Mustard
Jacket-Boiled Potatoes

Warm Gingerbread
Peaches and Cream

Serves 4.

WORK PLAN: Prepare one 14-ounce package gingerbread mix according to label directions. Divide one 16-ounce can peach halves among 4 dessert dishes; chill, and serve with pouring cream. Scrub 1 pound small potatoes very well; do not peel. Boil potatoes in salted water for 20 minutes or until tender; drain, then toss in 2 tablespoons melted butter or margarine and ¼ cup chopped parsley. Keep potatoes warm while making Knockwurst and Winekraut (see recipe below). Serve knockwurst with spicy mustard.

Knockwurst and Winekraut

2 slices bacon, cut up
¼ cup chopped onion
one 16-ounce can or package
  sauerkraut, drained
½ cup dry white wine
½ cup beef broth
1 cup grated apple
2 teaspoons caraway seeds
4 large knockwurst

1. Fry bacon pieces in large skillet over medium heat until semi-cooked; add onion and cook 5 minutes longer, until onion is brown and tender.

2. Add drained sauerkraut, wine, beef broth, apple and caraway seeds; mix well. Reduce heat to low and simmer, covered, for 10 minutes.

3. Place knockwurst on top of sauerkraut. Cover and simmer 10 minutes longer.

**SPANISH
FIESTA**

Arroz con Pollo

Olive and Tomato Salad

Sherried Orange and Ginger
Dessert

Serves 4.

WORK PLAN: Prepare Arroz con Pollo (see recipe below). While chicken is simmering, prepare salad: In large salad bowl, combine 4 cups shredded lettuce, 2 cups tomato wedges and ½ cup each pitted black olives and stuffed olives; chill. Toss with ½ cup red wine vinegar salad dressing just before serving. To prepare dessert, layer 1½ pints orange sherbet and one 11-ounce can mandarin oranges, drained, in 4 dessert glasses; freeze. Just before serving, top each with a little of mixture of ¼ cup chopped crystallized ginger and 1 tablespoon grated orange rind; pour a little sweet sherry on top.

Arroz con Pollo

2½- to 3-pound broiler-
  fryer chicken, cut into
  serving pieces
½ cup flour
¼ cup vegetable oil
½ cup sliced onion
one 8-ounce can tomato
  sauce
1 cup chicken broth
¼ cup chopped parsley
1 tablespoon prepared spicy
  mustard
1 cup quick-cooking rice
¼ cup chopped pimiento

1. Wash chicken well under cold running water; pat dry with paper towels. In large, clean brown paper or plastic bag, shake chicken pieces, two at a time, in flour to coat well. Set chicken aside.

2. Heat oil in large skillet over medium heat; add chicken and sauté for about 10 minutes, turning to brown all sides. Add tomato sauce, chicken broth, parsley and mustard. Reduce heat to low and simmer, covered, for 30 minutes.

3. Add rice to skillet; stir to mix well and simmer, covered, 5 minutes longer. Sprinkle with pimiento.

MEMORIAL DAY MENU

Hot Bacon-Onion Salad

"Fried" Chicken

Lemony Green Beans
Hot Biscuits

Apricots with Cheesecake Sauce

Serves 4.

WORK PLAN: First prepare dessert: Divide one 20-ounce can apricot halves, drained, among 4 dessert glasses; pour 1 tablespoon almond liqueur (or 1 tablespoon apricot juice mixed with ¼ teaspoon almond extract) over each. Divide sauce made of one 3-ounce package cream cheese, softened, ½ cup heavy cream and 2 tablespoons confectioners' sugar among the 4 glasses. Prepare "Fried" Chicken (see recipe below). Meanwhile, prepare vegetable by cooking two 10-ounce packages frozen green beans according to label directions; drain, and toss with ¼ cup lemon juice and 1½ teaspoons grated lemon rind and keep warm. To make salad, chill 6 cups bite-size pieces spinach; fry 6 slices bacon, cut into 1-inch pieces, with ½ cup onion rings. Add ¼ cup vegetable oil and ¼ cup vinegar; heat and toss with spinach just before serving. While chicken stands at room temperature, microwave one 11-ounce package ready-to-eat biscuits (in package) on high setting for 1 minute. *Shown on page 66.*

"Fried" Chicken

2½- to 3-pound broiler-fryer chicken, cut into serving pieces

1 cup puffed rice cereal

one 2⅜-ounce package chicken coating mix

½ cup butter or margarine

1. Wash chicken well under cold running water; pat dry with paper towels. Set chicken aside.

2. Place rice cereal in plastic bag included in chicken coating mix and crush cereal into crumbs; add chicken coating mix. Add chicken, two pieces at a time; shake well to coat.

3. Place butter or margarine in 12 x 7 x 2-inch glass baking dish. Microwave on high setting for 2 minutes to melt.

4. Place chicken skin side down in dish with thicker parts toward outside edge. Cover dish with waxed paper. Microwave on high setting for 10 to 15 minutes.

5. Turn chicken pieces skin side up; microwave on high setting, uncovered, for 10 to 15 minutes or until chicken is fork-tender. Let stand for 3 minutes at room temperature before serving.

NOTE: For really crisp skin, place under broiler 6 inches from heat for 2 minutes.

SOUTH SEAS SUPPER

Hawaiian Chicken

Cellophane Noodles
Bean Sprout Salad

Butterscotch Pudding
Coconut Cookies

Serves 4.

WORK PLAN: For salad, rinse and drain one 16-ounce can bean sprouts; toss with one 8-ounce can water chestnuts, drained and sliced, one 4-ounce can mushroom slices, drained, and ½ cup red wine vinegar salad dressing. Place in lettuce-lined bowl; chill. Make dessert by preparing one 3¾-ounce package instant butterscotch pudding mix according to label directions; divide among 4 individual dessert dishes and chill. Serve with coconut cookies. Make Hawaiian Chicken (see recipe below). Cook two 2-ounce packages cellophane noodles according to label directions.

Hawaiian Chicken

4 chicken breast halves, skinned and boned

¼ cup flour

2 tablespoons butter or margarine

one 10-ounce package frozen Hawaiian-style vegetables

one 8-ounce can pineapple chunks

2 tablespoons brown sugar

1 tablespoon soy sauce

¼ teaspoon ginger

1. Wash chicken breast halves under cold running water; pat dry with paper towels. Cut chicken into ¾-inch cubes; toss in flour.

2. Melt butter or margarine in large skillet over medium heat; add chicken cubes and sauté for about 5 minutes, turning to brown all sides. Reduce heat to low and cook 3 minutes longer.

3. Add Hawaiian-style vegetables, undrained pineapple chunks, brown sugar, soy sauce and ginger; stir to mix well. Continue cooking until vegetables are crisp-tender, about 3 minutes, stirring constantly to blend well.

MAHARAJAH DINNER

Curried Beef-Tomato Bouillon

Indian Chicken

Spinach and Onion Salad

Bananas in Coconut and Honey

Serves 4.

WORK PLAN: Prepare Indian Chicken (see recipe below). Mix 4 cups bite-size pieces spinach with 1 cup thin onion rings; chill. Toss with ⅓ cup garlic dressing just before serving. To make dessert, slice 2 large bananas and toss with 2 tablespoons lemon juice. Layer in 4 parfait glasses with shredded coconut, drizzling warm honey between each layer; chill. Prepare soup by combining 1½ cups spiced tomato juice, one 10½-ounce can beef bouillon and 1 teaspoon curry powder; heat mixture thoroughly.

Indian Chicken

4 chicken breast halves

1¾ cups water

one 6¾-ounce box long-grain and wild rice mix

½ cup currants or raisins

one 10¾-ounce can cream of chicken soup

⅓ cup dry white wine

⅓ cup water

paprika

1. Wash chicken breast halves under cold running water; pat dry with paper towels. Set chicken aside.

2. Bring 1¾ cups water to boiling point in medium saucepan over high heat. Stir in rice, contents of seasoning package and currants or raisins.

3. Pour rice mixture into lightly greased, shallow 2-quart oblong baking dish. Place chicken breasts skin side up on rice.

4. In small bowl, beat together chicken soup, wine and ⅓ cup water; pour mixture over chicken breasts. Sprinkle with paprika. Bake at 425° F for 35 minutes.

CASUAL DINING JAPANESE STYLE

Japanese Chicken and Steak

Rice

Japanese Vegetables

Sherbet-Filled Melon

Serves 4.

WORK PLAN: Prepare Japanese Chicken and Steak and Japanese Vegetables (see recipes below). Prepare 1 cup uncooked long-grain rice according to label directions. To make dessert, cut 2 tiny cantaloupes crosswise in half and scoop out seeds; chill melon. Just before serving, fill centers of melon halves with 1½ pints lemon sherbet; serve melon immediately.

Japanese Chicken and Steak

1 pound chicken breast halves, skinned and boned

1 pound sirloin steak

¼ cup vegetable oil

DIPPING SAUCE

½ cup dry sherry or sake

½ cup soy sauce

1 tablespoon sugar

¼ teaspoon powdered ginger, or 1 teaspoon finely chopped ginger root

1. Wash chicken well under cold running water; pat dry with paper towels. Wipe steak with damp paper towels. Cut chicken into 1-inch cubes; cut steak into ¼-inch-thick strips.

2. Heat oil in large skillet over medium heat; add chicken and beef and sauté until tender and lightly browned on all sides, about 4 minutes.

3. Meanwhile, make dipping sauce by combining sherry or sake, soy sauce, sugar and ginger in small saucepan. Bring to boiling point over low heat.

4. To serve, divide meat among 4 heated plates; divide dipping sauce among 4 small bowls.

Japanese Vegetables

¼ cup vegetable oil

1 cup sliced red onion

1 cup julienne strips zucchini

one 16-ounce can bean sprouts, rinsed and drained

¼ cup sesame seeds

¼ cup soy sauce

1. Heat oil in large skillet over medium heat; add onion and sauté until crisp-tender, about 2 minutes, stirring constantly.

2. Add zucchini; cook for 1 minute, stirring constantly. Add bean sprouts; cook until vegetables are crisp-tender and hot, about 2 minutes, stirring constantly.

3. Sprinkle vegetables with sesame seeds and soy sauce; stir to mix.

**RUSTIC
FRENCH DINNER**

Cornish Game Hens au Vin

Tiny Boiled Potatoes
Buttered Peas

Quick Mocha Mousse

Serves 4.

WORK PLAN: Prepare Cornish Game Hens au Vin and Quick Mocha Mousse (see recipes below). Peel 1 pound new potatoes and cut into quarters; boil in salted water for 15 minutes or until tender, then toss with ¼ cup chopped parsley and 2 tablespoons butter or margarine. Cook two 10-ounce packages frozen peas according to label directions; toss with 2 tablespoons butter or margarine.

Cornish Game Hens au Vin

2 Cornish game hens, quartered

¼ cup flour

2 slices bacon, cut into ½-inch pieces

2 tablespoons butter or margarine

1 clove garlic, crushed

½ cup chopped parsley

one 16-ounce jar whole white onions, drained

2 cups dry red wine

2 cups beef broth

1. Wash game hen quarters under cold running water; pat dry with paper towels. Sprinkle hens with flour; rub into all surfaces.

2. Fry bacon in large heavy skillet or saucepan over medium heat until crisp. Remove from pan with slotted spoon and set aside.

3. Melt butter or margarine in bacon fat in skillet; add game hen quarters and sauté for about 10 minutes, turning to brown all sides. Add garlic, 2 tablespoons of the parsley, the drained onions, wine and beef broth.

4. Reduce heat to low and simmer, covered, for 35 minutes or until game hens are tender. Serve in shallow soup bowls and sprinkle with remaining parsley.

Quick Mocha Mousse

one 3¾-ounce package
  instant chocolate pudding
  and pie filling
1 teaspoon instant coffee
2 cups heavy cream
1 tablespoon Grand
  Marnier or brandy
  (optional)
2 tablespoons sugar
chocolate sprinkles

1. Blend pudding mix and instant coffee in large bowl. Stir in 1 cup of the cream; add Grand Marnier or brandy if desired. Using electric mixer at low speed, beat mixture until smooth and thickened, about 2 minutes.

2. Using electric mixer at high speed, beat remaining cream in medium bowl until stiff peaks form. Fold half of whipped cream into mocha mixture. Divide mixture among 4 serving dishes.

3. Top each serving of mousse with remaining whipped cream sweetened with sugar; decorate with chocolate sprinkles. Chill until serving time.

**END-OF-THE-WORKDAY
DINING**

Ham-Horseradish
Appetizers

**Diced Chicken with
Broccoli**

Rice and Walnut Sauté

Fresh Fruit Platter

Serves 4.

WORK PLAN: Prepare appetizers by spreading each slice from ½ pound precooked ham with 2 teaspoons Dijon-style mustard and ½ teaspoon prepared horseradish; roll up jelly-roll fashion. Place 2 rolls on each of 4 individual salad plates and garnish with watercress sprigs and tiny gherkins; chill until serving time. Cook 1 cup long-grain rice according to label directions. Heat 2 tablespoons oil in large skillet over medium heat; add ½ cup chopped walnuts and sauté briefly. Stir in cooked rice; keep warm. Prepare Diced Chicken with Broccoli (see recipe below). For dessert, serve a selection of green grapes, pears and oranges.

Diced Chicken with Broccoli

one 10-ounce package
  frozen broccoli spears
1 pound chicken breast
  halves, skinned and boned
2 tablespoons vegetable oil
2 cloves garlic, slivered
1 tablespoon soy sauce
¼ teaspoon ginger

1. Cook broccoli according to label directions, but for only half the recommended cooking time. Drain and cool.

2. Wash chicken well under cold running water; pat dry with paper towels. Cut chicken into ¾-inch cubes.

3. Heat oil in large skillet, electric skillet or wok; add garlic and stir-fry for 1 minute. Discard garlic. Add chicken cubes; stir-fry for about 1 minute, constantly separating cubes.

4. Stir in soy sauce and ginger. Add broccoli spears; stir-fry until broccoli is crisp-tender and hot, about 3 minutes.

**SPRING
SUNDAY SUPPER**

Turkey-Rice Supreme

Broccoli Spears
Waldorf Salad

Warm Gingerbread with
Lemon Sauce

Serves 4.

WORK PLAN: Make one 14-ounce package gingerbread mix according to label directions. Then make salad: Mix 1½ cups apple slices, 1½ cups thinly sliced celery and ½ cup broken walnuts with ½ cup each mayonnaise and sour cream; place in lettuce-lined salad bowl and chill. Prepare Turkey-Rice Supreme (see recipe below). Cook two 10-ounce packages broccoli spears according to label directions. At dessert time, make Lemon Sauce by heating two 5-ounce individual-size cans lemon pudding with ½ cup heavy cream.

Turkey-Rice Supreme

1⅓ cups water

1⅓ cups quick-cooking rice

one 1½-ounce package onion soup mix

one 8-ounce can water chestnuts, drained and sliced

one 4-ounce can mushroom pieces, drained

2 cups diced cooked turkey

2 tablespoons butter or margarine

1. Bring water to boiling point in 2-quart heatproof casserole over medium heat. Stir in rice and onion soup mix.

2. Stir in water chestnuts, drained mushroom pieces and turkey. Toss to mix well. Dot with butter or margarine. Heat at 325° F for 20 minutes to develop flavors.

◎ *TimeSaving Tip:* Build a stockpile of instant casserole toppings for those days when dinnertime comes on in a rush. Convenient canned or packaged foods can add crunch and color to your main dish. Prechopped walnuts, almonds or pecans add zest to a casserole based on last night's roast. Crumbled potato chips, packaged stuffings and coarsely crumbled cracker crumbs are ideal substitutes for buttered bread crumb toppings. You can use unsweetened crisp cereals right out of the box, too. Have a variety of preshredded cheese—both mild and sharp—on hand to sprinkle on an entrée as a quick, savory addition. Sliced, drained water chestnuts can do double duty in and on top of all sorts of casseroles, as can salted or unsalted sunflower seeds.

COOL SEAFOOD MEAL

Honeydew Cocktail

Swedish Shrimp Salad

Crisp Rye Crackers

Banana Rum Cream

Serves 4.

WORK PLAN: Make Banana Rum Cream by preparing one 3¾-ounce package banana instant pudding and pie filling according to label directions. Fold in 1 banana, thinly sliced, and 2 tablespoons dark rum or orange juice. Divide among 4 dessert glasses and sprinkle with toasted coconut; chill. Prepare Swedish Shrimp Salad (see recipe below) and serve with rye crackers. Scoop flesh from seeded small honeydew melon with tiny melon baller; toss melon balls with 1 teaspoon each grated orange rind and grated lemon rind. Divide melon among 4 serving glasses; chill. Just before serving, pour champagne or ginger ale over melon.

Swedish Shrimp Salad

½ **pound medium shrimp, shelled and deveined**

one 10-ounce package frozen peas, thawed

one 8½-ounce can asparagus tips, drained

1 cup sliced mushrooms

4 cups fresh spinach leaves

½ **cup heavy cream**

⅓ **cup mayonnaise**

¼ **cup chili sauce**

1 tablespoon snipped dill

1. In small saucepan, cook shrimp in simmering salted water until tender, about 5 minutes. Remove shrimp to colander and cool quickly under cold running water; chill.

2. Combine thawed peas, drained asparagus tips and mushrooms. Divide mixture among 4 salad plates lined with spinach leaves; chill.

3. Beat cream in small bowl until stiff; fold in mayonnaise and chili sauce.

4. To serve, arrange chilled shrimp on top of salad on salad plates. Top each with whipped cream dressing and sprinkle with dill.

SHRIMP LOVERS' SPECIAL

Marinated Mushrooms and Peppers

Shrimp in Spice Sauce

Garlic Rice
Stir-Fry Zucchini

Lemon Sherbet with Apricot-Plum Wine Sauce

Serves 4.

WORK PLAN: To prepare appetizer, drain one 6-ounce can sliced mushrooms; combine mushrooms with ½ cup each julienne strips marinated red and green peppers. Toss with ¼ cup Italian-style dressing; divide among 4 lettuce-lined salad plates and chill. Next, prepare dessert by dividing 1½ pints lemon sherbet among 4 parfait glasses; freeze. Just before serving, pour a little of ½ cup apricot preserves blended with ¼ cup plum wine or dry sherry over each. Cook 1 cup long-grain rice according to label directions, adding 1 clove garlic, crushed, to water; keep warm. Prepare zucchini: Melt 2 tablespoons butter or margarine in large skillet over medium heat; add 4 cups julienne strips zucchini, 1½ teaspoons salt and ¼ teaspoon pepper and stir-fry until crisp-tender, about 4 minutes. At the same time, prepare Shrimp in Spice Sauce (see recipe below). *Shown on page 65.*

Shrimp in Spice Sauce

¼ cup vegetable oil

one 16-ounce package
  frozen shrimp

1 cup sliced onion

¼ teaspoon pepper

3 tablespoons ketchup

1 tablespoon soy sauce

1 tablespoon Worcestershire
  sauce

1 tablespoon cornstarch

1 tablespoon water

1. Heat oil in large skillet over medium heat; add frozen shrimp, onion and pepper and sauté for 2 to 3 minutes, until shrimp are cooked and onion is crisp-tender.

2. Add ketchup, soy sauce and Worcestershire sauce; stir and cook 1 minute longer.

3. Blend cornstarch and water; stir into skillet. Cook until mixture is thickened, about 1 minute, stirring constantly.

**NO-TIME-TO-SPARE
TUNA FRY**

Tomato Juice

Stir-Fry Tuna

Crisp Chinese Noodles
Crisp-Tender Celery

Peach and Raspberry Parfait

Serves 4.

WORK PLAN: Start by preparing dessert: Layer 1½ pints raspberry sherbet and one 16-ounce can cling peach slices, drained, in 4 parfait glasses; freeze. Next, divide 3 cups spicy tomato juice among 4 glasses; add lemon wedges and cucumber stick stirrers and chill. Lightly wrap crisp noodles from two 5-ounce cans in foil; heat in 300° F oven while making Stir-Fry Tuna (see recipe below). At the same time, heat 2 tablespoons oil in large skillet; add 4 cups thinly sliced celery, 1½ teaspoons each salt and celery seeds and ¼ teaspoon pepper, and stir-fry until celery is crisp-tender.

Stir-Fry Tuna

1 tablespoon vegetable oil

1 cup diced peeled apple

1 cup thin onion rings

two 7-ounce cans tuna,
  drained

2 teaspoons curry powder

¼ teaspoon dry mustard

one 10-ounce package
  frozen peas

1 cup golden raisins

1 cup cashews

¼ cup dry vermouth

1. Heat oil in large skillet over medium heat; add apple and onion and stir-fry until crisp-tender, about 1 minute.

2. Add tuna, stirring to flake; stir in curry and dry mustard. Add frozen peas, golden raisins, cashews and vermouth. Cook until mixture is very hot and well blended, about 5 minutes, stirring constantly to prevent scorching.

EGGS TO THE RESCUE

Cream of Mushroom Soup

Frittata

Hash Browns
Watercress-Spinach Salad
Double Orange Sherbet

Serves 4.

WORK PLAN: First, combine 2 cups each watercress sprigs and bite-size spinach leaves in large salad bowl; chill. Just before serving, toss with ¼ cup Italian-style salad dressing. To prepare dessert, divide 1½ pints orange sherbet among 4 parfait glasses. Make sauce for sherbet by blending ¾ cup orange marmalade and 2 tablespoons each lemon juice and water in small saucepan; heat just before serving. Prepare one 10¾-ounce can cream of mushroom soup according to label directions; keep warm. Cook one 16-ounce polybag frozen hash brown potatoes according to label directions. Prepare Frittata (see recipe below.)

Frittata

1 medium onion, peeled and quartered

1 medium-size green pepper, seeded and quartered

2 tablespoons butter or margarine

8 eggs

¼ cup heavy cream

¼ cup grated Parmesan cheese

¼ teaspoon pepper

1 large tomato, thinly sliced

¼ cup chopped parsley

1. With steel all-purpose blade in place in food processor, place onion and green pepper in food processor bowl. Chop finely by turning machine on and off for 5 seconds.

2. Melt butter or margarine in large skillet over low heat; add onion and green pepper and sauté until tender, about 4 minutes, stirring constantly.

3. Place eggs, cream, grated cheese and pepper in processor bowl. Process for 1 to 2 seconds to blend; pour into skillet.

4. Cook until bottom is set, about 2 to 3 minutes, stirring occasionally during first minute of cooking. Cover top surface with tomato slices; cook 1 minute longer, then sprinkle with parsley. Cut into wedges to serve.

SPEEDY SOUP AND SALAD

Liver Dumpling Soup

Deviled Egg Salad

Hot Crisp Rolls
Green Beans Italian

Almond Ice Cream

Serves 4.

WORK PLAN: Prepare 6 hard-cooked eggs for Deviled Egg Salad. Drain two 16-ounce cans whole green beans; toss beans with ⅓ cup Italian-style salad dressing and chill. To make dessert, divide 1½ pints vanilla ice cream among 4 dessert dishes; sprinkle each with 1 tablespoon toasted slivered almonds and freeze. Prepare Liver Dumpling Soup (see recipe below). Finish making Deviled Egg Salad (see recipe below) and heat 4 ready-to-serve rolls to serve with it.

Liver Dumpling Soup

½ pound beef liver

2 slices whole wheat bread, quartered

1 medium onion, peeled and quartered

2 tablespoons parsley sprigs

¾ cup flour

1 egg

½ teaspoon salt

¼ teaspoon pepper

two 10½-ounce cans beef broth

2 cups water

4 slices bacon

1. Wipe liver well with damp paper towels; peel off and discard membrane from outer edge of slices. Cut liver into 2-inch-long strips.

2. With steel all-purpose blade in place in food processor, place bread, onion and parsley in processor bowl. Chop coarsely by rapidly turning machine on and off for 10 seconds.

3. Add liver to processor bowl; process for 20 seconds to chop. Add egg, salt and pepper; process for 15 seconds to form a smooth batter.

4. Bring beef broth and water to boiling point in medium saucepan over medium heat. Dip a tablespoon into the boiling liquid to heat. Fill the spoon with liver mixture and dip again into boiling broth; dumpling will leave spoon immediately. Repeat procedure until liver mixture is used up. Reduce heat to low and simmer, covered, for 15 to 20 minutes.

5. Meanwhile, fry bacon in small skillet over medium heat until crisp. Drain on paper towels; crumble. Divide soup among 4 bowls; sprinkle with bacon.

Deviled Egg Salad

2 stalks celery, cut into 1-inch pieces

6 hard-cooked eggs, quartered

½ cup mayonnaise

2 tablespoons snipped fresh or frozen chives

1 tablespoon cider vinegar

½ teaspoon salt

¼ teaspoon dry mustard

¼ teaspoon Worcestershire sauce

3 to 4 drops hot pepper sauce

1 small head Boston lettuce

2 tablespoons mild paprika

2 tablespoons chopped parsley

1. With steel all-purpose blade in place in food processor, place celery in processor bowl; process for 5 seconds to chop.

2. Add eggs, mayonnaise, chives, vinegar, salt, dry mustard, Worcestershire sauce and hot pepper sauce. Chop by rapidly turning machine on and off for 5 seconds.

3. Arrange lettuce leaves on 4 individual salad plates. Divide salad among plates; sprinkle with paprika and parsley. Chill until serving time.

A CHIC
LITTLE SUPPER

Liverwurst Pâté
Wheat Crackers

Puffy Omelet Newburg

Shoestring Potatoes
Asparagus

Baked Melba Peaches

Serves 4.

5 **eggs, separated**
¼ **cup flour**
¼ **cup milk**
½ **teaspoon salt**
¼ **teaspoon pepper**
two 6½-**ounce packages**
 frozen lobster Newburg

WORK PLAN: Prepare dessert by placing peach halves from one 16-ounce can in lightly greased baking dish; fill center of each half with 1 tablespoon raspberry jam and place dish on lower shelf in 375° F oven. Prepare Puffy Omelet Newburg (see recipe below), placing on upper oven shelf. Heat shoestring potatoes from two 3½-ounce cans in covered casserole in oven beside peaches. Prepare two 10-ounce packages frozen asparagus spears according to label directions. Prepare appetizer by arranging 2 or 3 thin slices liverwurst, 2 or 3 gherkins and some wheat crackers on each of 4 serving plates.

Puffy Omelet Newburg

1. Preheat oven to 375° F.

2. In large bowl, beat egg yolks and flour until smooth; slowly stir in milk, salt and pepper.

3. Using electric mixer at high speed, beat egg whites in another large bowl until very stiff. Gently fold into egg yolk mixture. Spoon into well-greased 8-inch pie plate; bake for 20 minutes or until browned and puffy.

4. Meanwhile, heat lobster Newburg in top of double boiler over simmering water. Cut omelet into wedges to serve, with lobster Newburg alongside.

QUICK
CONTINENTAL
DINNER

Antipasto Platters

Spinach-Cheddar Quiche

Mushroom-Tomato Sauté

**Topsy-Turvy Black Forest
 Cake**

Serves 4.

WORK PLAN: To prepare appetizer, divide ½ pound each sliced salami and sliced liverwurst among 4 individual lettuce-lined salad plates; add 5 or 6 green and black olives and some tiny gherkins to each, and chill. Prepare Topsy-Turvy Black Forest Cake, then Spinach-Cheddar Quiche (see recipes below). Meanwhile, melt ¼ cup butter or margarine in large skillet over medium heat; add 4 cups thinly sliced mushrooms, 2 cups halved cherry tomatoes, and 1 teaspoon each salt, basil and oregano, and sauté for 5 minutes.

Topsy-Turvy Black Forest Cake

half of 18½-ounce package
chocolate cake mix

half of 21-ounce can cherry
pie filling

2 tablespoons cherry-
flavored liqueur

1 cup heavy cream, stiffly
beaten

¼ cup semisweet chocolate
morsels

1. Prepare cake mix according to label directions, using half the quantity of milk and eggs listed in instructions. Reserve remaining mix for later use.

2. Spread cherry pie filling in bottom of 9-inch glass pie plate. Reserve remaining cherry pie filling for later use.

3. Pour cake batter over cherry pie filling, spreading evenly to edge of pan. Microwave on 50% power for 7 minutes, rotating pan once.

4. Increase power to high setting; microwave for 3 minutes longer or until cake springs back when touched. Cool on wire rack for 5 minutes. Unmold onto serving platter; sprinkle with liqueur. Cool cake completely.

5. Frost cake with whipped cream. Sprinkle with chocolate morsels.

Spinach-Cheddar Quiche

one 9-inch frozen prepared
pie shell

1½ teaspoons soy sauce

one 10-ounce package
frozen chopped spinach

¼ cup grated onion,
drained

1 tablespoon grated
Parmesan cheese

¼ teaspoon nutmeg

3 eggs

¾ cup evaporated milk

2 cups grated sharp
Cheddar cheese

paprika

1. Transfer frozen pie shell from metal plate to 9-inch glass pie plate. Brush edge of crust with soy sauce for brown appearance. Prick crust thoroughly with fork. Microwave on high setting for 5 minutes or on 70% power for 7 minutes. Set aside to cool.

2. Place spinach in 1-quart glass casserole; cover dish with plastic wrap and microwave on high setting for 5 minutes. Drain very well; stir in drained onion, Parmesan cheese and nutmeg.

3. In medium bowl, beat together eggs and evaporated milk. Sprinkle 1 cup of the Cheddar cheese over bottom of pie shell; top with spinach mixture and remaining Cheddar cheese. Pour egg mixture over all; sprinkle with paprika.

4. Microwave on high setting for 6 to 8 minutes or on 70% power for 20 minutes. Rotate a quarter turn every 2 minutes during cooking process. Let stand at room temperature for 3 minutes before serving.

SPICY FIXIN'S

Melon Ball Salad

Curried Poached Eggs

Quick Apple Chutney

Coconut Custard Pie

Serves 4.

3 cups chopped unpeeled tart apples

½ cup chopped celery

¼ cup golden raisins

1 tablespoon snipped fresh or frozen chives

¼ cup brown sugar, firmly packed

2 tablespoons lemon juice

⅛ teaspoon ginger

⅛ teaspoon dry mustard

1½ cups uncooked long-grain rice

¼ cup chopped parsley

2 tablespoons butter or margarine

1 tablespoon instant minced onion

1 tablespoon flour

1½ teaspoons curry powder

¾ cup chicken broth

¼ cup milk

4 eggs

2 tablespoons vinegar

WORK PLAN: Thaw one 25-ounce frozen coconut custard pie at room temperature. Prepare appetizer by placing two unopened 12-ounce packages frozen melon balls in hot water to thaw. Divide melon balls among 4 individual serving dishes; chill. Prepare Quick Apple Chutney and Curried Poached Eggs (see recipes below).

Quick Apple Chutney

1. In serving bowl, mix together apples, celery, raisins and chives.

2. In small bowl, blend together brown sugar, lemon juice, ginger and dry mustard, stirring to dissolve sugar. Pour dressing over apple mixture; toss and serve with Curried Poached Eggs.

Makes 4 cups.

Curried Poached Eggs

1. Cook rice according to label directions; stir in parsley.

2. Meanwhile, melt butter or margarine in small saucepan over medium heat; blend in minced onion, flour and curry and stir for 1 minute.

3. Remove from heat; blend in chicken broth and milk. Reduce heat to low; return sauce to heat and bring to boiling point, stirring until thickened. Keep sauce warm.

4. In lightly greased medium skillet, poach eggs in 1 inch of simmering water containing vinegar until whites are set and yolks are still soft. Remove from skillet with slotted spoon and keep warm.

5. To serve, arrange hot parslied rice in ring on each of 4 serving plates. Set a poached egg in center of each and top with curry sauce.

**SOMETHING
DELICIOUSLY
DIFFERENT**

Potato Soup

**Fried Cheese Fingers and
Tomato Sauce**

Hot Spiced Cucumbers
Corn Niblets

Individual Trifles

Serves 4.

WORK PLAN: Prepare Individual Trifles (see recipe below). To pre-pare vegetables, peel, seed and dice 3 medium cucumbers; heat cu-cumbers in 2 tablespoons butter or margarine with ½ teaspoon pa-prika and 3 to 4 drops hot pepper sauce until hot and tender. Prepare one 16-ounce polybag frozen corn niblets according to label direc-tions. Keep vegetables warm. Prepare one 10¾-ounce can cream of potato soup according to label directions; keep warm. Make Fried Cheese Fingers and Tomato Sauce (see recipe below).

Individual Trifles

8 **pound-cake slices, ¼ inch
thick**

½ **cup apricot preserves**

¼ **cup sherry or orange
juice**

one 21-ounce can prepared
lemon pudding

1 **cup heavy cream**

2 **tablespoons sugar**

¼ **cup slivered almonds**

1. Sandwich together pound-cake slices, spreading 2 tablespoons preserves on one slice before topping with second slice. Cut each sandwich into ⅓-inch cubes; divide among 4 dessert glasses.

2. Sprinkle 1 tablespoon sherry or orange juice over cake cubes in each glass. Top each with one-fourth of the lemon pudding.

3. Just before serving, use electric mixer at high speed to beat cream in medium bowl until stiff, gradually beating in sugar. Divide among the dessert glasses. Sprinkle each with 1 tablespoon almonds.

Fried Cheese Fingers and Tomato Sauce

1-pound piece mozzarella
cheese

1 egg

1 tablespoon water

1 cup all-purpose flour

1 cup soda cracker crumbs

vegetable oil

one 8-ounce can tomato
sauce

1. Cut cheese into 16 fingers, approximately 3 x ½ x ½ inches.

2. In small bowl, beat together egg and water; pour onto platter. Place flour on another platter and cracker crumbs on a third platter. Roll cheese fingers in flour to coat evenly, then in egg mixture and finally in soda cracker crumbs.

3. Pour oil to ½-inch depth in large skillet; heat until oil is shim-mery. Fry cheese fingers eight at a time for 2 minutes, turning to brown all sides. Remove as cooked and keep warm; serve with hot tomato sauce.

Green Pea and Ham Soup

**Microwave Macaroni and
Cheese**

Relish Tray

Lemon Ice Cream Pie

Serves 4.

WORK PLAN: Prepare Lemon Ice Cream Pie (see recipe below). Then prepare relishes: Arrange 2 tomatoes, sliced, 2 zucchini cut into 2-inch-long julienne strips, ½ cup each black and green olives and 1 cup pickled hot green peppers on tray; chill. Prepare Microwave Macaroni and Cheese (see recipe below). While macaroni is standing at room temperature, prepare one 10¾-ounce can green pea and ham soup according to label directions; divide among 4 soup mugs and microwave on high setting for 1 minute.

Lemon Ice Cream Pie

½ cup butter or margarine

1½ cups crushed chocolate wafer crumbs

⅓ cup sugar

1 pint vanilla ice cream

1 pint lemon sherbet

½ cup heavy cream

2 tablespoons sugar

1. Melt butter or margarine in 9-inch glass pie plate by microwaving at high setting for 1½ to 2 minutes.

2. Mix in chocolate wafer crumbs and ⅓ cup sugar; press mixture to coat side and bottom of pie plate, forming crust. Microwave on high setting to firm crust. Chill in freezer.

3. Soften vanilla ice cream by placing in microwave oven on 10% power for 1 minute. Spread over bottom of chocolate crust; place in freezer. Soften lemon sherbet by placing in microwave oven on 10% power for 1 minute. Spread over vanilla ice cream; freeze.

4. Just before serving, use electric mixer at high speed to beat cream in small bowl until soft peaks form; sprinkle with 2 tablespoons sugar and continue beating until stiff. Swirl whipped cream over top of ice cream pie.

Microwave Macaroni and Cheese

2 cups elbow macaroni

2 tablespoons butter or margarine

¼ cup chopped green pepper

¼ cup chopped onion

2 cups grated sharp Cheddar cheese

¾ cup milk

½ teaspoon salt

½ teaspoon dry mustard

1. Cook macaroni according to label directions; drain.

2. Combine butter or margarine and green pepper in 2-quart glass casserole. Microwave on high setting for 2 minutes.

3. Stir in onion, grated cheese, milk, salt, dry mustard and cooked macaroni. Cover casserole with glass lid or plastic wrap.

4. Microwave at 70% power for 4 minutes; stir, re-cover and rotate a half turn. Microwave 4 to 5 minutes longer. Let stand, covered, at room temperature for 5 minutes.

Fast Summer Fare

Summer should be a lazy season, but most of us are still on the go. The kids need shuttling to their activities, the garden requires constant tending, your boss is on vacation and you're holding down the fort.

Relax. Take a breather with this selection of easy summer menus designed to help you keep cool when the weather isn't.

If a hot stove is unthinkable, why not choose the "No-Cook Patio Party": Summer Potato Soup (an instant iced vichyssoise) and Cold Corned Beef Salad, accompanied simply by rolls and olives. The kids will love the ice cream and cookies for dessert.

It's your turn to entertain and the thermometer is hovering near ninety? Easy does it. Just choose the "Celebration Supper" featuring a thirst-quenching Orange-Grapefruit Salad and Company Chicken Breasts, coolly cooked in a microwave oven and smothered with mushrooms and ham and cheese. The vegetables—Beans Almondine and Tomatoes Parmesan —are fit for a banquet, but don't tell anybody how simple they are to make. The tour de force is dessert: Open-Face Peach Pie topped with fresh whipped cream. And all in 45 minutes!

So when lazy days turn to dog days and the curl on your head wilts like yesterday's salad, catch a late swim at the pool. With the recipes in this chapter, supper will practically take care of itself.

ORIENTAL GRILL

Lemon-Chicken Soup

Teriyaki Steak

Crisp Noodles
Chinese Cabbage

Chilled Pineapple

Serves 4.

WORK PLAN: Prepare Teriyaki Steak (see recipe below). For dessert, cut a small pineapple into quarters. Cut flesh from each segment in one piece. Dice flesh and put back in shells; chill. Heat two 10¾-ounce cans chicken bouillon according to label directions, adding 4 to 6 lemon slices and 2 tablespoons lemon juice. Heat crisp noodles from two 5-ounce cans in small skillet over very low heat. Cook 4 cups finely shredded Chinese cabbage in ½ cup chicken broth until cabbage is crisp-tender.

Teriyaki Steak

1½ to 2 pounds boneless sirloin steak

1 cup soy sauce

⅓ cup dry sherry

¼ cup finely chopped onion

1 clove garlic, crushed

1 teaspoon ginger

1. Wipe steak with damp paper towels; cut meat into 1-inch cubes. In shallow baking dish, blend soy sauce, sherry, onion, garlic and ginger. Place meat cubes in marinade; let stand at room temperature for at least 30 minutes, turning frequently.

2. Preheat broiler.

3. Remove meat from marinade; reserve marinade. Place meat on 4 metal skewers. Broil 2 inches from heat, turning once and cooking 2 minutes per side. Brush with a little marinade while cooking.

COUNTRY-STYLE MEAL

Pan-Braised Round Steaks

Spinach Noodles
Cauliflower Parmesan

Fresh Strawberry Yogurt Dessert

Serves 4.

WORK PLAN: Prepare Pan-Braised Round Steaks (see recipe below). Meanwhile, prepare dessert: Beat 2 cups heavy cream until stiff; beat in 2 tablespoons confectioners' sugar. Fold in one 8-ounce container strawberry yogurt and 1 cup thinly sliced fresh strawberries. Divide mixture among 4 dessert dishes; chill. Cook two 10-ounce packages frozen cauliflower according to label directions; toss with 2 tablespoons grated Parmesan cheese. Cook one 16-ounce package spinach noodles according to label directions.

Pan-Braised Round Steaks

4 eye round steaks, ½ to ¾
  inch thick
¼ cup flour
¼ cup vegetable oil
2 cups spicy tomato juice
1 beef bouillon cube
1 teaspoon oregano
¼ teaspoon pepper
1 cup thin onion rings
2 tablespoons cornstarch

1. Wipe steaks with damp paper towels; sprinkle both sides of each steak with flour, rubbing well into surfaces.

2. Heat oil in large heavy skillet over medium heat; add steaks and sauté to brown, about 2 minutes per side.

3. Reduce heat to low; add tomato juice, bouillon cube, oregano and pepper. Simmer, covered, for 25 minutes. Place onion rings over steaks; simmer, covered, 10 minutes longer.

4. Place steaks with onion rings on serving platter. Blend cornstarch with a little cold water. Add to liquid in skillet and bring to boiling point, stirring constantly until thickened. Pour a little sauce over steaks; serve the rest alongside.

**SIMPLY WONDERFUL
SUPPER**

Mixed Fruit Cup

**Beef with Peppers and
Tomatoes**

Hot Herbed Rice

Chilled Lychees
Almond Cookies

Serves 4.

WORK PLAN: Prepare fruit cup: Peel and section 2 yellow grapefruit and 2 oranges; combine with 1 cup julienne strips apple. Divide among 4 individual serving dishes; chill. Next, prepare dessert: Divide two 16-ounce cans undrained lychees among 4 dessert glasses; chill, and serve with almond cookies. Prepare 1 cup long-grain rice according to label directions; stir in ¼ cup chopped parsley and keep warm. Prepare Beef with Peppers and Tomatoes (see recipe below).

Beef with Peppers and Tomatoes

1 pound beef chuck
¼ cup vegetable oil
2 cups thinly sliced red onions
2 cups cubed green pepper
2 tablespoons soy sauce
1 tablespoon dry sherry
1 tablespoon Worcestershire
  sauce
½ teaspoon sugar
¼ teaspoon pepper
1 tomato, cut into thin wedges

1. Wipe beef chuck well with damp paper towels; cut meat across grain into thin strips.

2. Heat oil in large skillet, electric skillet or wok; add beef and stir-fry for about 30 seconds, constantly separating pieces.

3. Add onions and green pepper; cook for 2 minutes, stirring constantly. Add soy sauce, sherry, Worcestershire sauce, sugar and pepper. Cook 1 minute longer, stirring constantly. Garnish with thin wedges of tomato.

FAST AND FESTIVE DINNER

Steaks Marchands de Vin

Cheese and Parsley Noodles
Glazed Onions

Fresh Fruit Salad

Serves 4.

WORK PLAN: First prepare dessert: In large bowl, combine 1 cup each sliced bananas, apples and pears with 1 cup grapes. Add 1 cup orange juice and chill; serve with stiffly beaten heavy cream. To prepare onions, heat ¼ cup firmly packed brown sugar and 1 tablespoon lemon juice in medium skillet over medium heat until sugar is melted; add 1 teaspoon coarsely crushed black pepper. Stir in two 16-ounce cans whole white onions, drained, turning to coat in glaze; keep warm. Cook one 16-ounce package egg noodles according to label directions; drain, then stir in ½ cup small curd cottage cheese and ¼ cup chopped parsley. Keep rice warm while preparing Steaks Marchands de Vin (see recipe below). *Shown on page 68.*

Steaks Marchands de Vin

4 beef cube steaks

2 tablespoons butter or margarine

2 tablespoons finely chopped green onion

1 tablespoon flour

½ cup beef broth

½ cup dry red wine

1 tablespoon Dijon-style mustard

1 tablespoon tomato paste

1 tablespoon lemon juice

¼ cup chopped parsley

1. Wipe cube steaks well with damp paper towels. Melt butter or margarine in large skillet over medium heat; add steaks and brown, about 2 minutes per side. Remove steaks to heated serving platter; keep warm.

2. Add green onion to drippings in skillet; sauté for 2 minutes or until tender. Stir in flour; cook 1 minute longer. Slowly stir in beef broth and wine. Bring to boiling point, stirring constantly. Stir in mustard, tomato paste and lemon juice. Pour over steaks; sprinkle with parsley.

STEAK AND EGGS SUPPER

Chilled Beet Soup

Sliced Beef and Scrambled Eggs

Stir-Fried Peppers

Watermelon Compote

Serves 4.

WORK PLAN: Start by preparing soup: Blend one 16-ounce can julienne beets, one 10½-ounce can beef broth and ¼ cup lemon juice; chill. At serving time, divide among 4 soup bowls; top each serving with 2 tablespoons sour cream and 1 tablespoon snipped fresh dill. To prepare dessert, cut flesh from watermelon into 1-inch chunks to measure 4 cups; divide among 4 dessert bowls. Pour ¼ cup orange juice over each portion and top each with a little grated orange rind; chill until serving time. Prepare Sliced Beef and Scrambled Eggs (see recipe below). At the same time, heat 2 tablespoons oil in large skillet and stir-fry 4 cups julienne strips green pepper with 1½ teaspoons salt and ¼ teaspoon pepper.

Sliced Beef and Scrambled Eggs

½ pound sirloin steak,
  ½ inch thick

1 tablespoon cornstarch

2 tablespoons water

1 tablespoon dry sherry

1 tablespoon soy sauce

½ teaspoon ginger

¼ cup vegetable oil

½ cup thinly sliced green
  onions

5 eggs, beaten

1. Wipe steak well with damp paper towels; cut meat across grain into thin strips. In medium bowl, blend cornstarch, water, sherry, soy sauce and ginger. Stir in beef to coat well; marinate at room temperature for 30 minutes, then remove from marinade.

2. Heat 2 tablespoons of the oil in large skillet, electric skillet or wok; add beef and stir-fry for about 30 seconds, constantly separating pieces. Remove from pan and set aside.

3. Pour drippings from skillet and wipe pan clean. Heat remaining 2 tablespoons oil in same skillet; add green onions and stir-fry for 10 seconds. Add beef strips; pour beaten eggs over beef. Reduce heat to low and cook until eggs are thickened, shiny, moist and tender. Serve immediately.

**EASY
OUTDOOR EATING**

Cold Sliced Roast Beef
Platter

Yogurt-Vegetable Relish

Crisp Club Rolls

Festive Summer Cake

Serves 4.

WORK PLAN: Prepare Yogurt-Vegetable Relish and Festive Summer Cake (see recipes below). Wrap 4 store-bought club rolls in foil and heat at 300° F until crisp. Arrange 1½ pounds sliced roast beef on platter and garnish with parsley sprigs; chill until serving time.

Yogurt-Vegetable Relish

1 cup unflavored yogurt

2 tablespoons lemon juice

2 tablespoons finely
  chopped green onion

1 tablespoon snipped fresh
  dill, or 1 teaspoon dried dill

1 cup diced green pepper

1 cup thinly sliced radishes

1 cup diced, seeded, pared
  cucumber

1. In medium bowl, blend yogurt, lemon juice, green onion and dill. Gently stir in green pepper and radishes; chill quickly in freezer. Chill diced cucumber separately.

2. To serve, drain any liquid from cucumber; fold cucumber gently into yogurt mixture.

Festive Summer Cake

one store-bought angel food cake

one 8-ounce can crushed pineapple

1 cup butter or margarine, softened

¾ cup confectioners' sugar

3 egg yolks

1 teaspoon almond extract

½ cup chopped pistachio nuts

1 cup heavy cream

½ cup toasted slivered almonds

1. Cut angel food cake into 3 even layers. Drain juice from pineapple; sprinkle juice over each layer. Place bottom layer on serving platter.

2. Using electric mixer at high speed, beat together softened butter or margarine, ½ cup of the confectioners' sugar, the egg yolks and almond extract in medium bowl. Spread butter mixture over bottom and middle layers.

3. Spread pineapple on top of butter mixture on bottom layer; set middle layer in position. Sprinkle pistachio nuts on top of butter mixture. Set top layer in position.

4. Using electric mixer at high speed, beat cream in large bowl until soft peaks form. Sprinkle in remaining ¼ cup confectioners' sugar. Beat until cream is stiff.

5. Frost top and sides of cake with whipped cream. Sprinkle almonds on top. Chill in refrigerator or freezer until serving time.

SUPPER FOR SWIMMERS

Melon Wedges with Lemon

Barbecued Beef Buns

Baked Beans
Cole Slaw

Speedy Lemon Pie

Serves 4.

WORK PLAN: Prepare melon by cutting cantaloupe or honeydew into 4 wedges; remove seeds and cut flesh of each wedge into bite-size pieces. Return pieces to shells. Cut 4 lemon wedges to go alongside; place melon and lemon on 4 individual serving plates and chill. Make dessert by preparing one 3¾-ounce package instant lemon pie filling according to label directions; spoon into an 8-inch prepared graham cracker crust. Top with refrigerator dessert topping; chill. Heat baked beans from two 16-ounce cans in medium saucepan over low heat; keep warm. Make Barbecued Beef Buns (see recipe below). Meanwhile, prepare cole slaw by mixing 4 cups shredded cabbage, 1 cup mayonnaise, 2 tablespoons celery seed and 1½ teaspoons salt.

Barbecued Beef Buns

1 pound ground beef

½ cup finely chopped green pepper

½ cup finely chopped celery (with leaves)

1 tablespoon instant minced onion

¾ cup prepared barbecue sauce

4 hamburger buns, split and toasted

1. Sauté ground beef, green pepper and celery in large skillet over low heat for 4 to 5 minutes, stirring constantly. Drain surplus fat from skillet.

2. Stir minced onion into beef mixture, mixing well; stir in barbecue sauce. Simmer, covered, for 10 to 15 minutes or until meat is tender. Serve over toasted hamburger buns.

COMPANY HAMBURGER FARE

Biftek Haché

Pommes Frites
Green Beans Vinaigrette

Strawberry Tarts Almondine

Serves 4.

WORK PLAN: Prepare Strawberry Tarts Almondine (see recipe below). Oven-fry half of one 32-ounce polybag frozen French fries according to label directions. Cook two 10-ounce packages frozen whole green beans according to label directions; drain and toss with 2 tablespoons each butter or margarine, red wine vinegar and grated Parmesan cheese. Keep beans warm while preparing Biftek Haché (see recipe below).

Strawberry Tarts Almondine

one 3¾-ounce package vanilla pudding and pie filling

2 cups milk

½ cup chopped almonds

1 tablespoon rum

4 prepared pastry tart shells

1 pint fresh strawberries, washed and hulled

1 cup red currant jelly

½ cup heavy cream

1. Prepare pudding and pie filling using 2 cups milk according to label directions. Pour half of prepared pudding into two 6-ounce custard cups; chill and use another day for dessert. Stir ¼ cup of the chopped almonds and the rum into remaining pudding.

2. Pour flavored pudding into pastry shells; arrange washed, hulled strawberries on top of each, stem side pressed into pudding.

3. Heat currant jelly in small saucepan over low heat until jelly is melted; spoon over strawberries to glaze. Chill until serving time.

4. Just before serving, use electric mixer at high speed to beat cream in medium bowl until stiff. Swirl over tops of tarts; sprinkle with remaining ¼ cup chopped almonds.

Biftek Haché

¼ cup butter or margarine

½ cup chopped onion

1 pound ground round beef

1 teaspoon salt

⅛ teaspoon pepper

1 egg, slightly beaten

½ cup flour

½ cup dry red wine

2 tablespoons chopped parsley

2 tablespoons snipped fresh or frozen chives

1. Melt 1 tablespoon of the butter or margarine in large skillet over medium heat; add onion and sauté until tender, about 3 to 4 minutes, stirring constantly.

2. In large bowl, combine ground beef, salt, pepper, slightly beaten egg and sautéed onion with pan drippings; mix well. Shape into 4 patties about ¾ inch thick. Coat meat well on both sides with flour.

3. Melt 2 tablespoons of the butter or margarine in same skillet over medium heat; add hamburgers and brown, 2 to 6 minutes per side. Remove to heated serving platter; keep warm.

4. Pour drippings from skillet. Pour wine into skillet; bring to boiling point over low heat, stirring to deglaze pan. Add remaining 1 tablespoon butter or margarine, the parsley and chives. Pour sauce over hamburgers.

HONG KONG SKILLET DINNER

Beef Chow Mein

White Rice

Fresh Pineapple and Melon Wedges

Serves 4.

WORK PLAN: Prepare 1 small pineapple and 1 small seeded melon by cutting into wedges. Cut flesh of each wedge into bite-size pieces; return pieces to shells and chill. Prepare Beef Chow Mein (see recipe below). Prepare long-grain rice for 4 servings according to label directions; serve with Beef Chow Mein.

Beef Chow Mein

1 pound ground beef

4 cups thinly sliced celery

1 cup thinly sliced onion

one 16-ounce can bean sprouts

1 cup beef broth

3 tablespoons soy sauce

3 tablespoons cornstarch

¼ teaspoon pepper

1. Slowly brown ground beef in large skillet over low heat for 4 to 5 minutes, stirring constantly to break meat into small pieces. Remove from skillet with slotted spoon and set aside.

2. Drain all but 2 tablespoons drippings from skillet. Add celery and onion to drippings in skillet and sauté over medium heat for 2 minutes, stirring constantly. Drain bean sprouts, reserving liquid. Stir bean sprouts into celery-onion mixture; reduce heat to low.

3. Combine bean sprout liquid, beef broth and soy sauce. In small bowl, blend cornstarch and pepper with liquid until smooth.

4. Pour liquid into mixture in skillet. Bring to boiling point over medium heat, stirring constantly until mixture thickens; stir in meat. Reduce heat to low and simmer, covered, for 15 minutes.

SUNBELT
SUPPER

Chilled Sherried Consommé

Fast Dinner Chili

Lettuce Wedges with Blue
Cheese Dressing

Instant Custard Dessert

Serves 4.

1 pound ground beef

½ cup chopped green
   pepper

one 15-ounce can tomato
   puree

¼ cup instant minced
   onion

1 tablespoon chili powder

1 teaspoon salt

1 teaspoon oregano

¼ teaspoon pepper

¼ teaspoon cumin

one 15½-ounce can red
   kidney beans, drained

one 5-ounce package taco
   chips

WORK PLAN: Begin by preparing dessert: Sprinkle 2 teaspoons dark brown sugar over bottom of each of four 6-ounce custard cups. Prepare one 3¾-ounce package instant vanilla custard dessert mix according to label directions and divide among custard cups; chill. Add 2 tablespoons sherry or lemon juice to two 10½-ounce cans beef consommé; chill. Make Fast Dinner Chili (see recipe below). While chili cooks, cut 1 small head iceberg lettuce into 4 wedges; place a wedge on each of 4 salad plates, pour blue cheese dressing over each and chill until serving time.

Fast Dinner Chili

1. Slowly brown ground beef in large skillet over low heat, stirring constantly to break meat into small pieces. Add green pepper; continue to cook, stirring constantly, for 3 minutes or until green pepper is soft.

2. Blend in tomato puree, minced onion, chili powder, salt, oregano, pepper and cumin. Simmer, covered, for 15 minutes.

3. Stir in drained kidney beans; simmer 5 to 10 minutes longer or until beans are very hot. Serve with taco chips.

TimeSaving Tip: When time is of the essence, look for a main dish recipe that uses ingredients that require a minimum of preparation, like the chili that appears on this page. One pound of ground chuck beef cooks rapidly in its own fat and can be stretched with the addition of canned beans and tomatoes. (Be sure the ground chuck you buy is bright red; look for the last-day-of-sale date on the package if dating laws are in operation in your area.) Entrées like this Fast Dinner Chili take no longer than 25 minutes to cook; the short cooking time means energy savings, too!

SUMMER SUPPER ESPAÑOL

Avocado Halves with Herb Dressing

Spanish Pie

Mixed Bean Casserole

Rainbow Sherbet
Rolled Cookies

Serves 4.

WORK PLAN: Prepare dessert by dividing ½ pint each orange, lemon and lime sherbert among 4 individual parfait glasses, arranging in layers; freeze, and serve with store-bought rolled cookies. Cut 2 avocados in half, remove pits, squeeze a little fresh lemon juice on each half to keep color, pour herb dressing into each cavity and chill. Make Spanish Pie (see recipe below). Mix together one 16-ounce can sliced green beans, one 15½-ounce can red kidney beans and one 15-ounce can lima beans; heat on top of stove or in oven.

Spanish Pie

1 **pound ground beef**

½ **teaspoon salt**

¼ **teaspoon pepper**

1½ **cups cooked quick-cooking rice**

one 12-ounce can Spanish **tomato sauce**

½ **cup water**

¼ **cup finely chopped green pepper**

1 **tablespoon instant minced onion**

1 **tomato, sliced**

1. In medium bowl, combine ground beef, salt and pepper. Press mixture into lightly greased 9-inch pie plate to form bottom "crust."

2. In another bowl, mix together cooked rice, tomato sauce, water, green pepper and minced onion. Pour over meat. Arrange tomato slices on top of sauce.

3. Bake pie at 400° F for 25 to 30 minutes, until meat and sauce bubble and meat is tender. Let stand for 3 to 4 minutes before cutting into wedges to serve.

BEACH-DAY DINNER

Grapefruit Halves

Skillet Macaroni and Beef

Chopped Broccoli
Banana Salad

Brownies

Serves 4.

WORK PLAN: Cut 2 grapefruit in half and section them; chill. Make salad: Place a lettuce leaf cup on each of 4 salad plates; fill each with 1 thinly sliced banana tossed with 1 tablespoon chopped unsalted peanuts. Top each with 1 tablespoon mayonnaise and chill. Prepare Skillet Macaroni and Beef (see recipe below). Prepare and bake one 15½-ounce package brownie mix according to label directions. Meanwhile, cook two 10-ounce packages frozen chopped broccoli according to label directions.

Skillet Macaroni and Beef

1 pound ground beef

one 28-ounce can tomatoes

¼ cup finely chopped onion

¼ cup finely chopped green pepper

¼ cup finely chopped parsley

1 teaspoon salt

1 cup uncooked elbow macaroni

one 4-ounce package shredded Cheddar cheese

1. Brown ground beef in large skillet over medium heat for 4 to 5 minutes, stirring to break meat into small pieces. Drain surplus fat from skillet.

2. Add undrained tomatoes, onion, green pepper, parsley and salt to beef, stirring to break tomatoes into small pieces. Stir in macaroni.

3. Reduce heat to low and simmer, covered, until macaroni is just tender, about 20 minutes, stirring occasionally. Sprinkle cheese over meat mixture; stir until just melted.

AFTER RUSH-HOUR SPECIAL

Cream of Shrimp Soup

Meat-Stuffed Tomatoes

Buttered Noodles
Minted Peas

Coconut Cream Cake

Serves 4.

WORK PLAN: Remove one 17-ounce coconut cream cake from freezer to thaw. Prepare Meat-Stuffed Tomatoes (see recipe below). Prepare two 10-ounce packages frozen peas according to label directions; drain, and add 1 tablespoon crumbled mint leaves. Meanwhile, prepare one 16-ounce package thin egg noodles according to label directions; drain, and toss with 2 tablespoons butter or margarine. Then heat one 10¾-ounce can cream of shrimp soup according to label directions.

Meat-Stuffed Tomatoes

6 large ripe tomatoes

1 teaspoon sugar

1 pound ground beef

⅓ cup quick-cooking rice

1 tablespoon dried parsley

2 teaspoons instant minced onion

½ teaspoon salt

½ teaspoon thyme leaves

1 tablespoon dry unseasoned bread crumbs

1 tablespoon butter or margarine

chopped parsley (optional)

1. Slice small section off base of each tomato to make it stand evenly. Cut ½-inch slice off tops of tomatoes; use teaspoon to remove pulp. Set pulp aside. Arrange tomato shells in greased baking pan; sprinkle cavities with sugar. Set aside.

2. Brown ground beef in medium skillet over medium heat for 3 to 4 minutes; drain surplus fat from skillet. Add rice, parsley, minced onion, salt and thyme leaves to beef; stir in reserved pulp. Simmer mixture for 10 minutes, stirring occasionally.

3. Fill tomato shells with meat mixture. Sprinkle with bread crumbs and dot with butter or margarine. Bake at 450° F for 10 minutes or until tomatoes are very hot and skin is slightly wrinkled. Sprinkle with parsley if desired.

NO-COOK PATIO PARTY

Summer Potato Soup

Cold Corned Beef Salad

Warm Dinner Rolls
Black and Green Olives

Coffee Ice Cream
Vanilla Wafers

Serves 4.

WORK PLAN: Prepare Cold Corned Beef Salad (see recipe below). For soup, puree one 10¾-ounce can cream of potato soup, one 10¾-ounce can chicken broth, ½ cup sour cream and ¼ cup chopped onion in electric blender at high speed. Stir in ¼ cup snipped fresh chives; chill. Prepare dessert by dividing 1½ pints coffee ice cream among 4 dessert dishes; freeze, and serve with packaged vanilla wafers. Wrap 4 store-bought dinner rolls in foil; heat at 300° F until warm. Serve rolls and a selection of olives with main course. *Shown on page 67.*

Cold Corned Beef Salad

1 **cup thin red onion rings**

1 **cup thinly sliced pared cucumber**

⅓ **cup garlic salad dressing**

½ **cup heavy cream**

¼ **cup prepared horseradish, drained**

2 **tablespoons brown sugar**

¼ **teaspoon salt**

1½ **pounds sliced precooked corned beef or pastrami**

1. In medium bowl, combine onion rings, cucumber slices and garlic dressing. Chill in refrigerator.

2. In another medium bowl, beat cream until stiff; fold in drained horseradish, brown sugar and salt. Chill in refrigerator for 30 minutes or in freezer until very cold.

3. To serve, remove onion rings and cucumber from salad dressing. Arrange corned beef or pastrami in rows on large platter with a row of onion rings and cucumber slices between each. Serve chilled horseradish-cream mixture alongside.

MENU ITALIANO

Veal Scaloppine

Linguine
Grated Zucchini Parmesan
Romaine Salad

Peaches in Marsala

Serves 4.

WORK PLAN: First prepare dessert: Peel 4 ripe peaches; cut in half, pit and place 2 halves in each of 4 individual dessert dishes. Pour ⅓ cup Marsala wine over each; chill. (Or use one 16-ounce can cling peach halves, drained.) Chill 4 cups bite-size pieces romaine lettuce in salad bowl; toss with ⅓ cup oil and vinegar dressing just before serving. Prepare vegetable by melting 2 tablespoons butter or margarine in medium skillet over low heat; add 4 cups grated zucchini, 1 teaspoon salt and ¼ teaspoon each pepper and nutmeg and sauté until zucchini is tender. Sprinkle with ¼ cup grated Parmesan cheese. Cook one 8-ounce package linguine according to label directions; keep warm while making Veal Scaloppine (see recipe below).

Veal Scaloppine

4 veal cutlets

2 tablespoons flour

½ teaspoon salt

¼ teaspoon pepper

¼ cup butter or margarine

½ cup dry white wine

1 envelope beef powder
  concentrate

¼ cup water

1 cup thinly sliced fresh
  mushrooms, or one
  3-ounce jar sliced
  mushrooms, drained

¼ cup chopped parsley

1. Wipe veal cutlets with damp paper towels. Place each cutlet between two sheets of waxed paper; using a wooden mallet or rolling pin, pound to ¼-inch thickness (or have your butcher do this). Sprinkle both sides of veal cutlets with flour seasoned with salt and pepper.

2. Melt 2 tablespoons of the butter or margarine in large skillet over low heat; add veal and sauté until tender and brown, 2 minutes per side, adding more butter or margarine as necessary. Add wine; simmer for 1 minute. Remove veal to heated serving platter; keep warm.

3. Add beef concentrate, water and mushrooms to wine in skillet. Stir well to deglaze pan. Simmer, covered, for 2 minutes or until mushrooms are just tender. Pour over meat; sprinkle with parsley.

QUICK AND ZESTY SUPPER

Chilled Green Pea Soup

Spicy Ham and Rice

Bean Salad with Sesame Dressing

Lemony Apricots

Serves 4.

WORK PLAN: Start by preparing soup: In electric blender, puree one 11¼-ounce can green pea soup, 1 cup light cream or milk and ½ cup sour cream at high speed until smooth. Divide among 4 soup bowls. Spinkle each with 1 tablespoon snipped fresh or frozen chives; chill. To prepare dessert, divide one 20-ounce can apricot halves among 4 dessert dishes. Blend ¾ cup lemon marmalade with ¼ cup apricot juice and pour ¼ cup over each dessert; chill. Prepare Bean Salad with Sesame Dressing (see recipe below). Finally, prepare Spicy Ham and Rice (see recipe below).

Bean Salad with Sesame Dressing

two 10-ounce packages
  frozen string beans

3 tablespoons sesame seeds

2 tablespoons soy sauce

1 teaspoon sugar

1 teaspoon ginger

¼ teaspoon pepper

1. Cook string beans according to label directions; drain.

2. Meanwhile, combine sesame seeds, soy sauce, sugar, ginger and pepper in small bowl. Pour over hot beans and toss well; serve warm or chilled.

Spicy Ham and Rice

2 tablespoons vegetable oil

1 pound precooked ham, cut into julienne strips

1 cup chopped onion

one 10¾-ounce can tomato soup

1 cup water

1 cup quick-cooking rice

⅛ teaspoon red pepper flakes

1 tablespoon ketchup

1. Heat oil in large skillet over medium heat; add ham and onion and sauté for 2 minutes. Add tomato soup, water, rice and red pepper flakes; mix well.

2. Reduce heat to low and simmer, covered, until rice is tender, about 8 to 10 minutes. Stir in ketchup.

COLD SOUP FOR A HOT DAY

Chilled Ham and Curry Soup

Hearts of Lettuce Salad

Warm Brown-and-Serve Rolls

Pear Compote

Serves 4.

2 tablespoons butter or margarine

¼ cup finely chopped onion

¼ cup finely chopped celery

2 teaspoons curry powder

one 10¾-ounce can tomato soup

one 11¼-ounce can green pea soup

1½ cups chicken broth

2 cups finely diced precooked ham

½ cup sour cream

WORK PLAN: Prepare Chilled Ham and Curry Soup (see recipe below). For dessert, drain one 20-ounce can pear halves and divide pears among 4 dessert dishes. Pour ⅓ cup Burgundy wine or orange juice over each serving and sprinkle each with 1 tablespoon chopped crystallized ginger; chill. Prepare one 8-ounce package brown-and-serve rolls according to label directions. Cut 4 wedges from head of iceberg lettuce and place each on a salad plate. Top each with some dressing made by blending ½ cup mayonnaise with 1 tablespoon lemon juice and ¼ cup snipped fresh or frozen chives.

Chilled Ham and Curry Soup

1. Melt butter or margarine in medium skillet over medium heat; add onion and celery and sauté until tender, about 5 minutes, stirring constantly. Stir in curry; cook 2 minutes longer.

2. Place onion-celery mixture in blender container. Add tomato soup, green pea soup and chicken broth. Blend at high speed for 30 seconds or until smooth.

3. Pour into soup tureen; stir in ham. Place in freezer to chill until serving time, taking care mixture does not freeze.

4. To serve, divide soup among 4 large soup bowls and top each serving with sour cream.

**PERFECT PICNIC
FARE**

Honeydew Melon with
Ginger Sugar

Ham Salad

Tomatoes with Onion

Rye Bread

Sherry Carrot Cake

Serves 4.

WORK PLAN: Prepare Sherry Carrot Cake (see recipe below). While the cake is baking, prepare Ham Salad (see recipe below). Prepare melon by cutting a small honeydew into quarters. Remove seeds and cut flesh into bite-size pieces; return to shells and chill. Serve with 1 cup sugar blended with 1 tablespoon ginger sprinkled over all, and with lime or lemon wedges on the side. Cut 4 large tomatoes into thin slices and arrange in overlapping lines on serving platter; sprinkle with ¼ cup Italian-style salad dressing and 2 tablespoons finely sliced green onion. Wrap a ready-to-serve loaf of rye bread in foil; heat alongside baking Sherry Carrot Cake for 10 minutes. Serve rye bread with sweet butter.

Sherry Carrot Cake

2 medium carrots, peeled
and cut into 3-inch-long
pieces

one 16.1-ounce quick nut
bread mix

½ cup golden raisins

½ teaspoon cinnamon

¼ teaspoon nutmeg

¾ cup water

¼ cup sherry

1 egg

1. Preheat oven to 350° F.

2. With steel shredding blade in place in food processor, place carrot pieces in tube in processor lid. Shred carrots by pressing down pusher.

3. Add nut bread mix, raisins, cinnamon, nutmeg, water, sherry and egg to carrots in processor bowl. With steel all-purpose blade in place, process until just blended, about 3 to 4 seconds.

4. Pour batter into lightly greased 9 x 5 x 3-inch loaf pan. Bake for 45 minutes or until a cake tester inserted in center comes out clean. Cool on wire rack before slicing.

Ham Salad

1½ pounds precooked ham,
cut into 1-inch cubes

1 medium-size green
pepper, quartered

1 cup mayonnaise

1 tablespoon lemon juice

1 teaspoon celery seed

¼ teaspoon pepper

1 head Boston lettuce

½ cup sliced stuffed olives

1. With steel all-purpose blade in place in food processor, place ham and green pepper in food processor bowl. Coarsely chop mixture by turning machine on and off for 10 seconds.

2. Add mayonnaise, lemon juice, celery seed and pepper. Process for 1 second, just to mix. Divide salad among 4 lettuce cups made from Boston lettuce; top with olive slices. Chill.

**COLD
COOL-OFF
MENU**

Avocado-Grapefruit Platter

**Deviled Ham and Egg
Sandwiches**

Tossed Green Salad

Applesauce Mousse

Serves 4.

WORK PLAN: Arrange segments of 1 avocado and 2 yellow grapefruit in pattern on platter and swirl on dressing of ⅓ cup each mayonnaise and sour cream blended with 2 tablespoons chopped mint; chill. Prepare dessert by folding 2 egg whites, stiffly beaten, and ½ cup heavy cream, stiffly beaten, into sweetened applesauce from one 16-ounce jar. Divide among 4 dessert dishes and chill. Chill 4 cups bite-size salad greens in salad bowl; toss with ⅓ cup oil and vinegar dressing just before serving. Make Deviled Ham and Egg Sandwiches (see recipe below).

Deviled Ham and Egg Sandwiches

1 loaf crusty French or Italian bread

one 4½-ounce can deviled ham

2 tablespoons mayonnaise

4 eggs

¼ cup finely sliced green onion

2 tablespoons milk

1 tablespoon butter or margarine

2 tomatoes, thinly sliced

4 slices Swiss cheese, cut into julienne strips

1. Preheat broiler.

2. Cut crusty bread lengthwise in half; cut each piece crosswise in half (there will be 4 quarters).

3. In small bowl, blend deviled ham with mayonnaise. Spread mixture generously over cut side of all 4 pieces of bread. Place each on individual heatproof serving platter.

4. Beat together eggs, green onion and milk. Melt butter or margarine in medium skillet over low heat; add egg mixture and cook, stirring constantly, until eggs are scrambled, soft, shiny and moist.

5. Divide eggs among bread quarters. Cover each portion with 2 or 3 tomato slices and some strips of cheese. Broil 4 inches from heat, until cheese is just melted.

**HOSTESS-SAVER
SUPPER**

Papaya with Lime

Savory Vienna Pastry Shells

Stir-Fried Zucchini with Walnuts

Butter Pecan Ice Cream with Fudge Sauce

Serves 4.

WORK PLAN: First prepare dessert by dividing 1½ pints butter pecan ice cream among 4 dessert dishes; freeze. Then prepare papaya by cutting it into wedges; discard black pearl-like seeds. Cut flesh into bite-size pieces, return to shells and chill; serve with lime wedges. Prepare Savory Vienna Pastry Shells (see recipe below). Meanwhile, heat 2 tablespoons oil in large skillet; add 4 cups diagonally sliced zucchini and ½ cup walnut pieces and stir-fry until zucchini is crisp-tender, about 3 to 4 minutes. At dessert time, heat one 8-ounce jar fudge sauce to serve over ice cream.

Savory Vienna Pastry Shells

one 10-ounce package
  frozen patty shells

one 10¾-ounce can cream of
  mushroom soup

½ cup tomato juice

2 tablespoons sherry or
  lemon juice

2 to 3 drops hot pepper
  sauce

two 7-ounce cans Vienna
  sausages, drained

one 8½-ounce can peas,
  drained

1. Prepare frozen patty shells according to label directions. Meanwhile, blend mushroom soup, tomato juice, sherry or lemon juice and hot pepper sauce in medium saucepan.

2. Cut Vienna sausages into bite-size pieces; add to sauce along with drained peas. Cover and heat (but do not boil) over low heat for 10 minutes, stirring occasionally.

3. Spoon Vienna sausage mixture into hot patty shells; serve surplus filling alongside.

**DINNER PARTY
MENU**

Braunschweiger en Croûte

Sautéed Mushrooms
Watercress-Cucumber Salad

Fruit and Cheese Platter

Serves 4.

WORK PLAN: Prepare Braunschweiger en Croûte (see recipe below). Make salad by tossing together 4 cups watercress sprigs and 2 cups thinly sliced cucumbers; chill. Just before serving, toss with ⅓ cup oil and vinegar salad dressing. Melt 2 tablespoons butter or margarine in medium skillet over low heat; add two 8-ounce cans mushroom caps, drained, and sauté lightly. For dessert, arrange selection of fruit and cheese; let stand at room temperature for 30 minutes before serving.

Braunschweiger en Croûte

one 8-ounce package
  refrigerator crescent rolls

1 tablespoon prepared
  mustard

1-pound roll
  Braunschweiger, at room
  temperature

1 egg, beaten

1 tablespoon sesame seeds

1. Preheat oven to 400° F.

2. Unroll crescent roll dough on lightly floured board; press gently to seal perforations and make single sheet of dough. Spread dough lightly with mustard.

3. Place Braunschweiger in center of dough; brush edges with a little beaten egg. Fold dough over Braunschweiger, pressing sides and ends to seal.

4. Place roll seam side down on baking sheet; brush with remaining egg and sprinkle with sesame seeds. Bake for 20 to 25 minutes or until crust is brown and crisp. Serve in thick slices.

**SOMETHING LIGHT
FOR SUPPER**

Broiled Lemon Chicken

Hot Crisp Noodles
Snow Peas and Water
Chestnuts

Lychees in White Wine

Serves 4.

WORK PLAN: To prepare dessert, drain one 16-ounce can lychees, place in 4 dessert glasses, cover with white wine and chill. Then prepare Broiled Lemon Chicken (see recipe below). Cook two 10-ounce packages Chinese snow peas according to label directions, adding one 8-ounce can water chestnuts, drained and sliced. Wrap noodles from two 5-ounce cans crisp Chinese noodles in foil, and heat for 5 minutes in oven before serving with chicken.

Broiled Lemon Chicken

2½-pound broiler-fryer
chicken, quartered

2 **tablespoons lemon juice**

1 **teaspoon grated lemon
rind**

½ **teaspoon salt**

¼ **teaspoon pepper**

¼ **cup butter or margarine**

SAUCE

3 **tablespoons sugar**

1 **tablespoon cornstarch**

1 **cup chicken broth**

1 **tablespoon lemon juice**

1. Preheat broiler.

2. Wash chicken quarters under cold running water; pat dry with paper towels. Rub chicken skin well with 1 tablespoon of the lemon juice, the lemon rind, salt and pepper. Melt butter or margarine in small saucepan over low heat with 1 tablespoon lemon juice.

3. Broil chicken, skin side up, 4 inches from heat, 15 to 20 minutes per side or until tender. Baste frequently with butter-lemon mixture.

4. Meanwhile, make sauce by blending sugar and cornstarch with chicken broth in small saucepan. Bring to boiling point over low heat, stirring constantly. Stir in 1 tablespoon lemon juice.

5. Place chicken on platter. Pour lemon sauce over chicken.

⊚ *TimeSaving Tip:* For a quick carbohydrate change, ready-to-eat chow mein noodles, corn chips or canned potato sticks can be heated as directed and served as a crisp accompaniment to dishes like Broiled Lemon Chicken (above). When selecting pastas and rice to serve as side dishes, look for the ones that cook the fastest—angel hair or cellophane noodles, available at most supermarkets and in Oriental food stores, and quick-cooking rice are all time-savers. Fresh pasta is not only a scrumptious change from regular boxed pasta, it takes a fraction of the cooking time that the packaged pasta requires.

**CELEBRATION
SUPPER**

Orange-Grapefruit Salad

Company Chicken Breasts

Beans Almondine

Tomatoes Parmesan

Open-Face Peach Pie

Serves 4.

WORK PLAN: Transfer one 9-inch frozen pie shell from metal plate to 9-inch glass plate; brush edge of pastry with 2 teaspoons vanilla extract to brown crust. Microwave on high setting for 5 minutes; set aside to cool. Divide one 16-ounce jar orange and grapefruit fruit salad among 4 individual dishes; chill. Prepare Company Chicken Breasts (see recipe below). Meanwhile, fill cooled pie shell with one 32-ounce can cling peach slices, drained and tossed with 1 cup coarsely chopped golden raisins; just before serving, swirl ½ cup heavy cream, stiffly beaten with 2 tablespoons confectioners' sugar, over top. While chicken is standing at room temperature, mix one 16-ounce polybag cut green beans and ½ cup slivered almonds with ¼ cup water in 1-quart glass casserole; cover dish with plastic wrap and place in microwave oven. Place 4 large tomato halves, each sprinkled with 1 tablespoon grated Parmese cheese, on paper towels on floor of microwave. Microwave beans and tomatoes on high setting for 5 minutes.

Company Chicken Breasts

**4 chicken breast halves,
skinned and boned**

¼ cup butter or margarine

**one 10¾-ounce can golden
mushroom soup**

**one 3-ounce can sliced
mushrooms, drained**

**¼ cup dry sherry or
vermouth**

1 teaspoon basil

¼ teaspoon pepper

**¼ cup chopped precooked
ham**

**¼ cup grated Swiss or
mozzarella cheese**

1. Wash chicken breasts under cold running water; pat dry with paper towels. Set chicken aside.

2. Place butter or margarine in 12 x 7 x 2-inch glass baking dish. Microwave on high setting for 30 seconds, until butter or margarine is melted.

3. Roll chicken breasts in melted butter or margarine to coat; arrange in dish with thicker edges of chicken toward outside edges of dish. Cover dish tightly with plastic wrap. Microwave on high setting for 10 minutes.

4. In small bowl, mix together mushroom soup, drained mushrooms, sherry or vermouth, basil and pepper. Turn chicken over; pour sauce over all. Re-cover and continue to microwave on high setting for 6 to 8 minutes or until chicken is tender.

5. Sprinkle with ham and cheese; cover and let stand at room temperature for 5 minutes before serving.

MIDDLE EASTERN MENU

Chicken Pilaf

Dilled Green Beans
Greek Salad

Grapes with Honey-Yogurt Dressing

Serves 4.

WORK PLAN: Prepare Chicken Pilaf (see recipe below). Meanwhile, prepare dessert: Cut 4 cups seedless green grapes in half and toss with 1 cup unflavored yogurt and ½ cup honey; chill. Then prepare salad: Combine 4 cups shredded lettuce with one 8-ounce package feta cheese, crumbled, 1 cup tomato wedges and ½ cup pitted black olives; chill. Toss with ⅓ cup garlic dressing just before serving. Cook two 10-ounce packages cut green beans according to label directions; drain, and toss with ¼ cup snipped fresh dill or 2 tablespoons dried dill and 2 tablespoons butter or margarine.

Chicken Pilaf

2½- to 3-pound broiler-fryer chicken, cut into serving pieces

¼ cup butter or margarine

1 cup chopped onion

1 envelope chicken powder concentrate

1 clove garlic, crushed

¼ teaspoon cinnamon

one 6-ounce can tomato paste

¾ cup cold water

1 cup uncooked long-grain rice

¼ cup pine nuts or slivered almonds

2 cups boiling water

1. Wash chicken well under cold running water; pat dry with paper towels. Melt butter or margarine in large skillet over medium heat; add chicken and sauté for about 10 minutes, turning to brown all sides. Remove from skillet and set aside.

2. Add onion, chicken concentrate, garlic and cinnamon to drippings in skillet; sauté until onion is golden, about 3 to 4 minutes, stirring constantly.

3. Blend together tomato paste and cold water; stir into onion mixture. Return chicken to skillet; reduce heat to low and simmer, covered, for 5 minutes.

4. Stir in rice and pine nuts or almonds. Pour in boiling water, stirring constantly. Cover and simmer 20 to 25 minutes longer or until rice and chicken are tender.

CURRY IN A HURRY

Eggplant Caviar
Crackers

Quick Chicken Curry

Rice
Peanuts, Coconut, Chutney, Orange Slices

Lime Sherbet and Ginger

Serves 4.

WORK PLAN: Chill one 6-ounce can caponata (eggplant caviar); serve with crisp wheat crackers. Cook 1 cup long-grain rice according to label directions; keep warm. Arrange salted peanuts, toasted coconut, chutney and fresh orange slices in small bowls; these are *sambals* to mix with Quick Chicken Curry and rice. Divide 1½ pints lime sherbet among 4 dessert glasses; sprinkle each portion with 1 tablespoon chopped crystallized ginger, then freeze until dessert time. Make Quick Chicken Curry (see recipe below).

Quick Chicken Curry

4 chicken breast halves,
skinned and boned

¼ cup vegetable oil

½ cup chopped celery

¼ cup sliced green onion

2 teaspoons curry powder

one 10¾-ounce can cream of
celery soup

half of 2¾-ounce package
onion soup mix

1 cup water

1 tablespoon lemon juice

1. Wash chicken breast halves under cold running water; pat dry with paper towels. Cut chicken into ¾-inch cubes. Heat oil in large skillet over medium heat; add chicken cubes a few at a time and sauté for 5 minutes, turning to brown all sides. Remove chicken as browned, then return all chicken to skillet.

2. Stir celery, green onion and curry into chicken in skillet; sauté for 5 minutes or until vegetables are crisp-tender, stirring constantly.

3. In small bowl, beat together celery soup, onion soup mix, water and lemon juice. Pour over chicken-celery mixture; stir to mix well. Reduce heat to low and simmer, covered, for about 10 minutes or until chicken is tender and flavors have developed.

**QUICK-COOK
KEBABS**

Watercress-Cucumber Soup

Chicken Kebabs

Parslied Rice

Orange Sherbet with
Bittersweet Chocolate

Serves 4.

WORK PLAN: Make Chicken Kebabs (see recipe below). Prepare dessert by dividing 1½ pints orange sherbet among 4 dessert glasses; grate bittersweet chocolate heavily over sherbet and freeze. Cook 1 cup long-grain rice according to label directions; stir in ⅓ cup chopped parsley at end of cooking time. While rice is cooking, heat two 10¾-ounce cans chicken bouillon, ½ cup finely chopped, seeded, pared cucumber and ½ cup chopped watercress; keep warm.

Chicken Kebabs

4 chicken breast halves,
skinned and boned

2 green peppers

2 zucchini

MARINADE

1 cup bottled Italian-style
dressing

2 tablespoons sugar

¼ teaspoon garlic powder

1. Wash chicken breast halves under cold running water; pat dry with paper towels. Cut chicken into ¾-inch cubes. Seed green peppers and cut into ¾-inch cubes; cut zucchini into ½-inch slices.

2. To make marinade, beat together dressing, sugar and garlic powder in large bowl. Stir in chicken cubes, green pepper cubes and zucchini slices. Marinate at room temperature for at least 25 minutes or, preferably, overnight in refrigerator.

3. Preheat broiler.

4. Remove chicken and vegetables from marinade; reserve marinade. Arrange chicken cubes alternately with green pepper and zucchini on 4 large skewers. Broil 3 inches from heat for 10 to 15 minutes, turning frequently and basting with reserved marinade.

BEAT-THE-HEAT CHICKEN DINNER

Artichoke Salad

Sweet and Sour Chicken

Julienne Carrots and Celery

Strawberries in Currant Sauce

Serves 4.

WORK PLAN: Prepare dessert by combining 4 cups sliced fresh strawberries with ¾ cup red currant jelly blended with ¼ cup port wine or lemon juice; toss to combine, and chill in large dessert bowl. Next, make salad: Prepare one 10-ounce package frozen artichoke hearts and one 10-ounce package frozen peas according to label directions; drain and combine and, while hot, toss with ½ cup garlic dressing. Place on 4 lettuce-lined salad plates; chill. To prepare vegetable, cook 2 cups each julienne strips carrots and celery in boiling salted water until tender. Drain, then toss with ½ cup chopped parsley and 2 tablespoons butter or margarine; keep warm. Prepare Sweet and Sour Chicken (see recipe below).

Sweet and Sour Chicken

4 large chicken breast halves, skinned and boned

2 tablespoons vegetable oil

½ cup chopped onion

one 8-ounce can pineapple chunks

1 cup sweet pickle slices

2 tablespoons sugar

2 tablespoons vinegar

2 tablespoons soy sauce

1 tablespoon cornstarch

1 tablespoon water

1. Wash chicken well under cold running water; pat dry with paper towels. Cut chicken into 1-inch cubes. Heat oil in large skillet, electric skillet or wok; add chicken and stir-fry until lightly browned, about 2 minutes.

2. Add onion to pan; stir-fry 1 minute longer. Drain pineapple and reserve juice; add chunks to pan. Stir in sweet pickle slices, sugar, vinegar and soy sauce; stir-fry for 1 minute.

3. Blend cornstarch, water and reserved pineapple juice; stir into chicken mixture. Cook until mixture is thickened, about 1 to 2 minutes, stirring constantly.

DINNER FOR DROP-INS

Hot Parslied Beef Broth

Piquant Summer Chicken Salad

Toaster Corn Cakes
Zucchini Sticks

Chilled Pineapple Chunks

Serves 4.

WORK PLAN: Prepare Piquant Summer Chicken Salad (see recipe below). Divide one 20-ounce can pineapple chunks among 4 dishes and chill for dessert. Cut 3 medium zucchini into julienne strips and toss with ½ cup oil and vinegar dressing; chill. Prepare soup by heating one 10½-ounce can beef broth, ½ cup each water and sherry and ¼ cup chopped parsley. Heat 4 toaster corn cakes according to label directions.

Piquant Summer Chicken Salad

2 cups diced cooked chicken
1 cup finely diced celery
1 cup finely diced green
  pepper
1 cup seedless green grapes,
  halved
one 8-ounce can crushed
  pineapple, drained
½ cup mayonnaise
½ cup unflavored yogurt
½ cup chopped walnuts
lettuce leaves
mint sprigs

1. Toss chicken with celery, green pepper and halved green grapes.

2. In small bowl, blend drained pineapple, mayonnaise, yogurt and walnuts. Pour over chicken salad; toss gently to combine.

3. Chill salad for at least 30 minutes or until serving time. Arrange on lettuce-lined salad platter and garnish with mint sprigs.

**MUGGY DAY
MEAL**

Turkey and Bean Salad
Cole Slaw-Stuffed Tomatoes
Bread Sticks
Pistachio-Mint Ice Cream

Serves 4.

WORK PLAN: Start by making Turkey and Bean Salad (see recipe below). Cut ½-inch slice from top of each of 4 large beefsteak tomatoes to form lids; hollow out tomatoes. Fill each shell with one-fourth of a 16-ounce container of store-bought cole slaw; chill, and serve with bread sticks. Prepare dessert by dividing 1½ pints pistachio ice cream among 4 dessert dishes; freeze. Just before serving, beat 2 tablespoons crème de menthe or 1 teaspoon peppermint extract into 1 cup heavy cream, stiffly beaten; swirl over ice cream.

Turkey and Bean Salad

one 15½-ounce can red
  kidney beans, drained
1 cup diced cooked turkey
⅔ cup diced celery
⅓ cup sweet pickle relish,
  drained
¼ cup mayonnaise
2 tablespoons grated onion
1 tablespoon prepared mustard
4 hard-cooked eggs
romaine lettuce leaves

1. Toss together drained kidney beans, turkey, celery and drained pickle relish. Stir in mayonnaise, onion and mustard. Chill in refrigerator until serving time.

2. To serve, coarsely chop hard-cooked eggs; stir into salad. Place salad on lettuce-lined platter.

TOO-HOT-TO-COOK DELIGHT

Beef Bouillon on the Rocks

Fruit Salad with Turkey

Celery and Cucumber Sticks
Toasted Date Nut Bread

Raspberry Sherbet

Serves 4.

WORK PLAN: Prepare Fruit Salad with Turkey (see recipe below). Cut 4 stalks celery and 2 unpared cucumbers into 3- to 4-inch sticks; chill. Divide 1½ pints raspberry sherbet among 4 parfait glasses; freeze. Cut 4 slices from store-bought loaf of date nut bread. Cut slices into quarters and toast; keep warm. To make soup, mix two 10½-ounce cans beef bouillon, 1 teaspoon Worcestershire sauce and 6 drops hot pepper sauce; pour over crushed ice in 4 old-fashioned glasses and serve immediately.

Fruit Salad with Turkey

one 3-ounce package cream cheese

½ cup mayonnaise

½ cup heavy cream

one 16-ounce can fruit cocktail, drained

1 cup miniature marshmallows

¼ cup quartered maraschino cherries (optional)

mint sprigs

1½ pounds sliced precooked turkey roll

1. Using electric mixer at high speed, beat cream cheese and mayonnaise in medium bowl until softened and well blended.

2. Using electric mixer at high speed, beat heavy cream in small bowl until stiff. Fold into cream cheese mixture.

3. Chill cream cheese dressing, drained fruit cocktail, marshmallows and cherries in separate bowls. Just before serving, fold fruit cocktail, marshmallows and cherries into cream cheese dressing.

4. Mound in center of large salad platter; garnish with mint sprigs and surround with turkey slices.

TimeSaving Tip: During the summer, when heat and warm-weather activities cut down on the time you can spend in the kitchen, make it a habit to have two or three cans of soup chilling in the refrigerator to serve as cooling, instant appetizers. Condensed soups can be spiced and poured over ice, or thinned with milk, cream or chilled wine. Try icy chicken bouillon spiked with dry sherry; cream of asparagus soup thinned with lemon juice and sour cream; or cold tomato consommé mixed with chilled clam juice.

Shrimp Lovers' Special (*page 32*)

Memorial Day Menu (*page 26*)

No-Cook Patio Party (*page 52*)

Fast and Festive Dinner (*page 44*)

Gala Mexican Menu (*page 86*)

Last-Minute Highland Supper (*page 98*)

Double-Quick Dinner Deluxe (*page 118*)

Dinner for New Year's Eve (*page 134*)

**SOPHISTICATED
SEAFOOD SUPPER**

Blue Cheese and
Pumpernickel Hors
d'Oeuvres

Seafood Mousse

Chilled Zucchini and
Mushrooms

Fresh Peaches
Toasted Pound Cake Fingers

Serves 4.

WORK PLAN: Prepare Seafood Mousse (see recipe below). Toss together 2 cups each thinly sliced zucchini and mushrooms, and chill; just before serving, toss with dressing made by blending ⅓ cup olive oil, 2 tablespoons lemon juice, 1 teaspoon each salt, sugar and dry mustard and ¼ teaspoon pepper. Prepare hors d'oeuvres by spreading 8 slices pumpernickel bread with sweet butter. Top with thin slices of blue cheese, then thin radish slices. Cut hors d'oeuvres into quarters and serve sprinkled with freshly ground pepper. Cut one 9½-ounce packaged pound cake into slices; toast and cut into fingers. Serve with sliced fresh peaches.

Seafood Mousse

**one 16-ounce package
frozen white fish**

**one 3-ounce package lemon-
flavored gelatin**

1⅓ cups tomato juice

**one 3-ounce package cream
cheese, softened**

½ cup mayonnaise

**½ cup chopped green
pepper**

½ cup chopped celery

2 tablespoons lemon juice

**1 teaspoon Worcestershire
sauce**

½ teaspoon celery salt

1. Cook fish according to label directions. Drain off any liquid; cool fish and flake finely. Chill in freezer.

2. Place gelatin in blender container. Heat ⅔ cup of the tomato juice in small saucepan until very hot (do not boil); pour onto gelatin. Blend at high speed for 15 to 30 seconds or until gelatin is dissolved.

3. Add remaining ⅔ cup tomato juice, the cream cheese and mayonnaise. Blend at high speed for 30 seconds or until mixture is smooth.

4. Pour mixture into large bowl; stir in green pepper, celery, lemon juice, Worcestershire sauce and celery salt. Add flaked white fish.

5. Divide mixture among 4 individual soufflé dishes or custard cups. Chill mousse in freezer until serving time, taking care mixture does not freeze.

NOTE: If there is time to spare, chill Seafood Mousse in refrigerator.

TimeSaving Tip: If you're in a super hurry and forgot to take the fish out to thaw, don't despair—make an entrée that calls for flaked fish like the Seafood Mousse (above). Cook the frozen fillets in a solid block for 3 to 5 minutes longer than the package indicates. The cooked fish will be easy to flake for whatever main course you have in mind.

**PORCH-SITTERS'
SUPPER**

**Spinach Salad with
Crabmeat Dressing**

Avocado Platter
Crescent Rolls

Lemon Sherbet
Cinnamon Cookies

Serves 4.

one 16-ounce container
  small curd cottage cheese

½ cup diced celery

½ cup diced, seeded, pared
  cucumber

½ cup mayonnaise

¼ cup chopped onion

2 tablespoons lemon juice

4 cups fresh spinach leaves

DRESSING

1 cup mayonnaise

¼ cup chili sauce

2 tablespoons finely
  chopped onion

2 tablespoons horseradish,
  drained

one 6½-ounce package
  frozen crabmeat

WORK PLAN: Prepare one 8-ounce package refrigerator crescent rolls according to label directions; keep warm. Make Spinach Salad with Crabmeat Dressing (see recipe below). Divide 1½ pints lemon sherbet among 4 dessert dishes; freeze, and serve for dessert with store-bought cinnamon cookies. Cut 2 large avocados into thin wedges and arrange on serving platter; spoon ¼ cup Italian-style salad dressing over avocados and chill until serving time.

Spinach Salad with Crabmeat Dressing

1. In medium bowl, blend cottage cheese, celery, cucumber, ½ cup mayonnaise, ¼ cup chopped onion and the lemon juice.

2. Line large salad platter with washed and dried spinach leaves; mound cottage cheese mixture in center and chill until serving time.

3. To make dressing, blend 1 cup mayonnaise, the chili sauce, 2 tablespoons chopped onion and the drained horseradish in small bowl. Quickly thaw crabmeat in package under running water; drain well and flake into mayonnaise mixture. Chill until serving time; serve dressing alongside salad.

○ *TimeSaving Tip:* You've probably found that fresh spinach is often sandy and time-consuming to prepare; but don't waste time washing off each individual leaf. Instead, try this method of washing and drying: plunge the spinach into two or three bowls of cold water, wrap the leaves in a large, clean dish towel and shake them dry.

KEEP-YOUR-COOL MEAL

Two-Bean Tuna Salad

Garden Tomato Platter
Whole Wheat Fingers

Cranberry-Peach Tapioca

Serves 4.

WORK PLAN: Prepare Cranberry-Peach Tapioca, then prepare Two-Bean Tuna Salad (see recipes below). Next, cut 4 large tomatoes into thin slices; arrange in overlapping lines on serving platter, sprinkling with 1 teaspoon each salt and sugar, and ½ teaspoon pepper. Just before serving time, spread 4 to 8 whole wheat bread slices with sweet butter; cut slices into fingers.

Cranberry-Peach Tapioca

¼ cup quick-cooking
  tapioca

¼ cup sugar

¼ teaspoon ground cloves

2 cups cranberry juice

one 20-ounce can cling
  peach slices, drained

½ cup heavy cream

1. In medium saucepan, combine tapioca, sugar and cloves. Slowly blend in cranberry juice. Bring to boiling point over medium heat, stirring constantly until mixture thickens and tapioca is tender.

2. Dice drained peaches and fold into tapioca mixture. Stir to cool, and divide among 4 dessert dishes. Chill tapioca in freezer until serving time.

3. To serve, beat heavy cream until stiff and swirl over desserts.

Two-Bean Tuna Salad

one 7-ounce can tuna,
  drained

½ cup diced celery

½ cup mayonnaise

¼ cup sliced green onion

2 tablespoons lemon juice

1 tablespoon snipped fresh
  dill, or 1 teaspoon dried dill

1 teaspoon dry mustard

one 16-ounce can pinto
  beans, drained

one 16-ounce can wax
  beans, drained

½ cup garlic salad dressing

1. Flake drained tuna into medium bowl; stir in celery, mayonnaise, green onion, lemon juice, dill and dry mustard. Chill in freezer until serving time.

2. In another medium bowl, combine drained pinto and wax beans; toss with garlic dressing. Chill in freezer until serving time.

3. To serve, mound tuna mixture in center of large salad platter. Drain beans from salad dressing; place in a ring around tuna.

**SIMPLE SUNSET
SUPPER**

Oriental-Style Omelet

White Rice
Sweet-Sour Pineapple Relish

Sherried Plums

Serves 4.

WORK PLAN: Prepare dessert: Drain one 20-ounce can whole purple plums and divide fruit among 4 parfait glasses; spoon 2 tablespoons sweet sherry over each serving and chill. Prepare relish by combining one 16-ounce can pineapple chunks, drained, 1 cup thin radish slices and ¼ cup each brown sugar and cider vinegar; chill. Prepare 1⅓ cups quick-cooking rice according to label directions; keep warm while making Oriental-Style Omelet (see recipe below).

Oriental-Style Omelet

1 tablespoon cornstarch

1 tablespoon Chinese-style
brown seasoning sauce

1½ cups chicken broth

6 eggs

one 16-ounce can bean
sprouts, rinsed and well
drained

1 cup finely diced cooked
roast pork or precooked
ham

½ cup finely chopped onion

¼ cup finely chopped green
onion

¼ cup chicken broth

2 tablespoons soy sauce

1 teaspoon sugar

¼ cup vegetable oil

¼ cup chopped parsley

1. Blend cornstarch, brown seasoning sauce and a little of the 1½ cups chicken broth in small saucepan; mix until smooth. Blend in the rest of the 1½ cups chicken broth. Bring to boiling point over medium heat, stirring constantly until mixture thickens. Reduce heat to very low; cover and keep sauce warm while making omelet.

2. Beat eggs very well in large bowl; add bean sprouts, pork or ham, onion, green onion, ¼ cup chicken broth, the soy sauce and sugar. Beat to blend well.

3. Heat oil in very large skillet over medium heat until surface of oil ripples and has a very faint haze. Reduce heat to low; stir in egg mixture. Continue to stir with fork until eggs begin to set; cook 1 minute longer without stirring until bottom is golden and top surface is shiny and moist.

4. Fold omelet in half with large spatula; gently slide onto large heated serving platter. Pour a little sauce over omelet; sprinkle with parsley. Serve remaining sauce alongside.

**SATURDAY
STAY-HOME
SUPPER**

Cheddar Quiche

Tomato and Onion Sauté
Double Green Bean Salad

Chocolate Cake

Serves 4.

WORK PLAN: Prepare salad by combining one 16-ounce can cut green beans, drained, and one 16-ounce can lima beans, drained; chill. Just before serving, toss with ½ cup cucumber salad dressing. Prepare Cheddar Quiche (see recipe below). Melt 2 tablespoons butter or margarine in large skillet over low heat; add 2 cups tomato wedges, 2 cups thinly sliced onions, 1 teaspoon salt, 1 teaspoon sugar and ¼ teaspoon pepper and sauté until vegetables are tender, about 5 to 6 minutes. Serve store-bought chocolate cake for dessert.

Cheddar Quiche

1 cup grated sharp Cheddar cheese

one 7-inch frozen prepared pie shell

¼ cup chopped green onion

3 eggs

¾ cup evaporated milk or half-and-half

½ teaspoon salt

¼ teaspoon pepper

¼ teaspoon dry mustard

paprika

1. Preheat oven to 400° F.

2. Sprinkle grated cheese over bottom of pie shell; sprinkle green onion over cheese.

3. In medium bowl, beat eggs, evaporated milk or half-and-half, salt, pepper and dry mustard. Pour mixture over cheese and onion in pie shell. Sprinkle lightly with paprika. Bake for 30 minutes or until knife inserted in center of quiche comes out clean.

EASY SUMMER SCRAMBLE

Curried Beef Vegetable Soup

South of the Border Scramble

Broiled Eggplant and Tomato Slices

Fruit Platter

Serves 4.

one 16-ounce can tortillas

2 tablespoons butter or margarine

¼ cup chopped onion

¼ cup chopped green pepper

8 eggs

1 tablespoon milk

2 tablespoons chopped parsley

½ teaspoon salt

¼ teaspoon pepper

WORK PLAN: Prepare one 10½-ounce can beef vegetable soup according to label directions, adding ½ teaspoon curry powder; keep warm. Arrange fresh fruit on platter for dessert; chill. Next, place ½-inch-thick slices of eggplant and tomato on baking sheet; brush both sides of slices with oil and season with salt and pepper. Broil 4 inches from heat for 5 minutes; turn and broil 5 minutes longer. Meanwhile, prepare South of the Border Scramble (see recipe below).

South of the Border Scramble

1. Separate tortillas and fry a few at a time in large skillet according to label directions. Drain fried tortillas on paper towels; set aside and keep hot.

2. Melt butter or margarine in same skillet over low heat; add onion and green pepper and sauté until crisp-tender, about 1 to 2 minutes.

3. In medium bowl, beat eggs, milk, parsley, salt and pepper. Pour mixture over onion and green pepper; cook until set, stirring to scramble but keeping eggs shiny and slightly moist. Serve eggs over hot crisp tortillas.

TOSS-TOGETHER SUPPER

Curried Luncheon Meat

Egg and Beet Salad

Whole Wheat Rolls

Vanilla Ice Cream

No-Bake Cookies

Serves 4.

WORK PLAN: Prepare No-Bake Cookies and Egg and Beet Salad (see recipes below). Cut chilled luncheon meat from one 12-ounce can into julienne strips; toss with ½ cup mayonnaise, 2 tablespoons lemon juice, 1 teaspoon curry powder and ¼ teaspoon pepper. Place in lettuce-lined bowl and chill. Divide 1½ pints vanilla ice cream among 4 dessert dishes; freeze until ready to serve with cookies.

No-Bake Cookies

1 cup golden raisins

1 cup walnut pieces

1 cup dried apricot halves

1 cup pitted dates

one 3-ounce can flaked coconut

1 cup creamy peanut butter, softened

1. Finely grind combination of raisins, walnuts, apricots and dates in food processor or meat grinder.

2. Stir in coconut and peanut butter; press into 8 x 8 x 2-inch baking pan lined with foil. Chill in freezer; cut into 2-inch squares.

Makes 16.

Egg and Beet Salad

½ cup cider vinegar

2 tablespoons sugar

1 teaspoon dry mustard

1 teaspoon salt

one 16-ounce can sliced beets

chicory leaves

4 hard-cooked eggs, chilled

1. Stir together vinegar, sugar, dry mustard and salt in medium saucepan; heat over low heat just until sugar is dissolved. Remove from heat; add undrained beets. Chill in freezer until serving time.

2. To serve, remove beets from liquid; mound in center of chicory-lined platter. Cut chilled eggs with egg slicer and arrange slices around beets.

MIDSUMMER MEAL

Sardines Vinaigrette

Double Salad Platter

Herb Buttermilk Biscuits

Strawberries and Cream

Serves 4.

WORK PLAN: First drain two 3¾-ounce cans sardines packed in oil; arrange sardines and ½ cup thin red onion rings on 4 lettuce-lined salad plates. Pour 1 tablespoon red wine vinegar and oil dressing over each portion and chill. Prepare Double Salad Platter (see recipe below). Prepare one 8-ounce package refrigerator buttermilk biscuits according to label directions; 1 minute before end of baking time, brush with 2 tablespoons melted butter or margarine combined with ¼ teaspoon each crumbled thyme and sage. Divide ¾ cup sliced fresh strawberries among 4 dessert dishes; sprinkle each with 1 tablespoon sifted confectioners' sugar. Serve with pouring cream.

Double Salad Platter

1 pound potatoes, peeled
and diced

¼ cup mayonnaise

2 tablespoons snipped fresh
or frozen chives

one 10-ounce package
frozen peas

¼ cup oil and vinegar salad
dressing

¼ cup diced pimiento

¼ cup sliced black olives

4 hard-cooked eggs, sliced

1. Cook potatoes in boiling salted water for 10 minutes or just until tender. Cool under cold running water; drain thoroughly. Toss with mayonnaise and chives; chill.

2. Cook peas according to label directions; cool under cold running water and drain well. Toss with salad dressing, diced pimiento and sliced olives; chill.

3. To serve, mound potato salad in center of platter. Add half of eggs to pea salad and place remaining eggs around potato salad.

GARDEN VEGETABLE TABLE

Tomato-Basil Salad

Vegetable Cheese Casserole

Crusty French Bread
Buttered Cauliflower

Chocolate Mousse

Serves 4.

WORK PLAN: First prepare Chocolate Mousse (see recipe below). Prepare salad by arranging 1 large tomato, thinly sliced, on each of 4 individual salad plates. Sprinkle each with 1 teaspoon basil and 1 teaspoon sugar; chill, and serve with oil and vinegar. Cook two 10-ounce packages frozen cauliflower according to label directions. Drain, then toss with 2 tablespoons butter or margarine, 2 tablespoons grated Parmesan cheese and 1 teaspoon paprika; keep warm. Prepare Vegetable Cheese Casserole (see recipe below). Wrap a loaf of crusty French bread in foil; heat alongside casserole for last 5 minutes of cooking time.

Chocolate Mousse

one 6-ounce package
semisweet chocolate
morsels

4 eggs, separated

2 tablespoons rum, or 2
teaspoons rum extract

½ cup heavy cream

2 tablespoons sugar

1. Melt chocolate in top of double boiler over simmering water. Remove from heat; mix in egg yolks, blending well. Stir in rum or rum extract.

2. Using electric mixer at high speed, beat egg whites in large bowl until stiff. Gently fold into chocolate mixture. Spoon into 4 individual soufflé or dessert dishes; chill until serving time.

3. To serve, use electric mixer at high speed to beat cream in medium bowl until stiff, then beat in sugar. Swirl one-fourth of whipped cream on top of each serving of mousse.

Vegetable Cheese Casserole

2 tablespoons butter or margarine

6 cups julienne strips green pepper

2 cups thinly sliced onions

½ teaspoon salt

¼ teaspoon pepper

⅓ cup dry seasoned bread crumbs

one 8-ounce package Swiss cheese slices

1. Melt butter or margarine in large skillet over medium heat; add green pepper and onions and sauté until crisp-tender, about 5 to 8 minutes, stirring constantly. Sprinkle with salt and pepper; stir in bread crumbs.

2. Layer one-third of pepper mixture in lightly geased 8 x 8 x 2-inch baking dish; top with one-third of cheese slices. Repeat layers to use up vegetables and cheese, ending with cheese layer. Bake at 450° F for 10 minutes or until cheese is melted. Cut into fourths to serve.

FRUIT AND VEGETABLE DINNER DELUXE

Chilled Vegetable Juice

Banana-Cheese Mousse

Endive-Zucchini-Mushroom Salad

Blueberries and Walnut-Sugar Cream

Serves 4.

one 3-ounce package raspberry-flavored gelatin

¾ cup boiling water

½ teaspoon dry mustard

1½ cups small curd cottage cheese

1 cup mashed banana

2 tablespoons mayonnaise

2 tablespoons sugar

½ cup heavy cream, stiffly beaten

WORK PLAN: Prepare Banana-Cheese Mousse (see recipe below). Next, toss together 4 cups bite-size pieces endive and 2 cups each zucchini and mushroom slices. Just before serving with Banana-Cheese Mousse, toss with ½ cup oil and vinegar dressing. Divide vegetable juice cocktail from one 24-ounce can among 4 glasses; place celery stick in each and chill. For dessert, wash 2 pints fresh blueberries, removing stems; divide berries among 4 dessert dishes. Serve with topping of 1 cup heavy cream, stiffly beaten, mixed with ⅓ cup finely chopped walnuts and 2 tablespoons brown sugar.

Banana-Cheese Mousse

1. In medium bowl, blend gelatin, boiling water and dry mustard; stir well to dissolve gelatin. Chill in freezer until semi-set, about 20 minutes, taking care that mixture does not freeze.

2. Blend together cottage cheese, banana, mayonnaise and sugar. Blend gelatin into mixture; gently fold in stiffly beaten cream.

3. Divide mixture among 4 individual soufflé dishes or custard cups. Chill mousse in freezer until serving time, taking care that mixture does not freeze.

Short-Cut Fall Dinners

With the invigorating tang of autumn in the air, leaves crackling in the yard and wood smoke puffing up the chimney, appetites grow heartier and welcome back warm foods full of flavor. Red meats, pork and sausage take more prominence in your repertoire; filling vegetables like dried beans and golden squash seem appropriate again; and desserts reflect this cool-weather season.

During these busy back-to-school weeks, the dinner table is often the only meeting ground for the whole family. With these timesaving recipes you'll have the leisure to linger over three-course dinners with your family. They'll love your efficiency when you surprise them with dishes like Meat Crust Pizza and Caramel Baked Apples from "The Kids' Choice," and Tomato-Sherry Soup, Stuffed Acorn Squash, Skillet Mushroom and Corn Casserole and Cranberry Snow from the "Weekend Football Supper."

Besides an arresting assortment of everyday dinners from all over the world, you'll find meals for every mood and occasion. How about Quick-Fry Chicken and Gravy when you're rushing out to the movies or Speedy Pork with Raisin Sauce on homecoming weekend?

Take time to enjoy the fall colors and don't feel guilty about dinner. It'll be ready in no time thanks to the short-cut menus you'll find in this chapter.

LABOR DAY STEAK DINNER

Sherried Grapefruit Juice

Shredded Beef with Mushrooms

Orange Rice
Stir-Fried Spinach

Apple Coconut Cream

Serves 4.

WORK PLAN: Start by combining 3 cups unsweetened grapefruit juice and ½ cup sweet sherry or coconut cream; divide among 4 serving glasses and chill. To make rice, cook 1 cup long-grain rice according to label directions. At the same time, heat 1 tablespoon oil in medium skillet over medium heat; add ½ cup julienne strips orange rind and sauté for 3 to 4 minutes. Stir orange rind into cooked rice; keep warm. Heat 2 tablespoons oil in large skillet; add 4 cups bite-size pieces spinach and stir-fry until wilted. Keep spinach warm. Prepare dessert: Beat ½ cup heavy cream in medium bowl until stiff; fold in 1 cup sweetened applesauce and one 3-ounce can flaked coconut. Divide among 4 dessert glasses; chill. Make Shredded Beef with Mushrooms (see recipe below).

Shredded Beef with Mushrooms

½ **pound sirloin steak, ½ inch thick**

2 **tablespoons vegetable oil**

1 **tablespoon cornstarch**

2 **tablespoons soy sauce**

1 **tablespoon dry sherry**

2 **cups thinly sliced fresh mushrooms, or one 6-ounce can sliced mushrooms, drained**

¾ **cup thinly sliced green onions**

½ **teaspoon ginger**

1. Wipe steak well with damp paper towels; cut meat across grain into thin strips. Heat oil in large skillet, electric skillet or wok; add beef and stir-fry for about 30 seconds, constantly separating strips.

2. Blend cornstarch, soy sauce and sherry; stir into beef. Add mushrooms, green onions and ginger and stir-fry for 2 minutes, until mushrooms are just tender and mixture is hot.

MEAT AND POTATO LOVERS' SPECIAL

London Broil

Hash Brown Potatoes
Spicy Zucchini

Cream and Fruit Pie

Serves 4.

WORK PLAN: Prepare London Broil (see recipe below). Make dessert by beating 2 cups heavy cream until almost stiff, then beating in ¼ cup confectioners' sugar. Fold one 20-ounce can fruit cocktail, well drained, into whipped cream. Spoon mixture into an 8-inch prepared graham cracker pie shell; chill, and serve within 45 minutes. Prepare one 16-ounce package frozen hash brown potatoes according to label directions. Melt 2 tablespoons butter or margarine in medium skillet over medium heat; add 4 cups sliced zucchini and sauté until tender, about 4 to 5 minutes. Sprinkle zucchini with 1½ teaspoons salt, ¼ teaspoon pepper and ¼ teaspoon nutmeg.

London Broil

2-pound London broil, about 1½ inches thick

½ cup vinegar and oil salad dressing

¼ cup soy sauce

¼ cup honey

¼ cup lemon juice

1 teaspoon ginger

1. Wipe London broil with damp paper towels. Place meat in large shallow baking dish. Combine salad dressing, soy sauce, honey, lemon juice and ginger and pour over meat. Turn meat to cover with marinade; let stand at room temperature for 30 minutes, turning frequently.

2. Preheat broiler.

3. Remove meat from marinade; reserve marinade. Broil meat 4 inches from heat, 4 to 8 minutes per side. Brush meat frequently with marinade while cooking. Place on serving platter; slice diagonally into thin strips to serve.

BACK-TO-SCHOOL DINNER

Smothered Steaks

French Fries
Peas and Carrots

Blueberry Turnovers
Serves 4.

WORK PLAN: Bake one 12-ounce package frozen blueberry turnovers according to label directions. Place French fries from one 16-ounce polybag on baking sheet; thaw and crisp in oven according to label directions. Prepare Smothered Steaks (see recipe below). Meanwhile, cook two 10-ounce packages frozen peas and carrots according to label directions.

Smothered Steaks

2 tablespoons butter or margarine

2 cups julienne strips green pepper

1 cup thin onion rings

1 envelope beef powder concentrate

2 tablespoons dry sherry or red wine

1 tablespoon tomato paste

one 32-ounce package frozen chopped steaks (four 8-ounce steaks)

1. Preheat broiler.

2. Melt butter or margarine in medium skillet over medium heat; add green pepper strips and onion rings and sauté until crisp-tender, about 4 minutes, stirring constantly.

3. Stir in beef concentrate, sherry or red wine, and tomato paste. Reduce heat to low and simmer, covered, for 5 minutes, stirring occasionally; keep warm.

4. Broil steaks 4 inches from heat, 7 to 10 minutes per side. Place on serving platter. Smother with pepper-onion mixture.

OKTOBERFEST SPREAD

Königsberger Klops

Red Cabbage with Apples
Parslied Dumplings

Almond-Lemon Torte

Serves 4.

WORK PLAN: First prepare dessert: Split 2 store-bought 8-inch layer cakes horizontally in half to make 4 layers. Place 1 layer on serving platter and spread top with ¼ cup lemon marmalade; continue to assemble cake, spreading ¼ cup lemon marmalade between each layer. Frost with one 15-ounce can vanilla frosting blended with ¼ cup ground almonds and 1 teaspoon almond extract; chill. Heat one 20-ounce jar red cabbage according to label directions, adding 1 cup thinly sliced unpared apples; keep warm. Prepare Königsberger Klops (see recipe below). To make dumplings, mix 2 cups packaged biscuit mix with ¼ cup chopped parsley and ⅔ cup water to form a soft dough. Drop by tablespoonfuls into boiling salted water; when dumplings rise to surface, reduce heat to low and simmer, covered, for 10 minutes.

Königsberger Klops

1½ **pounds ground beef**

1 **cup soft fresh bread crumbs**

2 **eggs, beaten**

¼ **cup chopped parsley**

2 **tablespoons lemon juice**

1¾ **cups beef broth**

2 **tablespoons butter or margarine**

2 **tablespoons flour**

one 3-ounce jar capers, drained

1 **teaspoon salt**

¼ **teaspoon pepper**

1. In large bowl, combine ground beef, bread crumbs, beaten eggs, parsley and 1 tablespoon of the lemon juice; mix well. Shape into meatballs, each 1½ inches in diameter.

2. Bring beef broth to boiling point in large saucepan over medium heat; add meatballs and turn to coat in hot broth. Reduce heat to low and simmer, covered, for 10 to 15 minutes. Remove meatballs from broth with slotted spoon; place in serving dish and keep warm. Pour broth into glass measure.

3. Melt butter or margarine in same saucepan over medium heat; stir in flour. Cook until mixture bubbles, about 2 minutes, stirring constantly.

4. Remove from heat; blend in reserved beef broth. Return to heat; bring to boiling point, stirring constantly until mixture thickens. Stir in remaining 1 tablespoon lemon juice, the drained capers, salt and pepper. Simmer, covered, for 2 minutes; pour over meatballs.

EASY FAMILY SUPPER

Swedish Meatballs

Mashed Potatoes
Brussels Sprouts

Mandarin Orange-Pineapple
Sundaes

Serves 4.

WORK PLAN: Divide 1 pint vanilla ice cream among 4 dessert dishes. Divide one 11-ounce can mandarin oranges, drained, and one 5¼-ounce can pineapple chunks, drained, among ice cream servings; freeze. Make Swedish Meatballs (see recipe below). Meanwhile, prepare two 10-ounce packages frozen Brussels sprouts according to label directions, and make 4 servings instant mashed potatoes, beating in 2 additional tablespoons butter or margarine.

Swedish Meatballs

1 **pound ground beef**

⅓ **cup dry unseasoned bread crumbs**

1 **tablespoon instant minced onion**

½ **teaspoon salt**

¼ **teaspoon pepper**

¼ **teaspoon nutmeg**

1 **egg, beaten**

2 **tablespoons butter or margarine**

one 10¾-ounce can cream of **mushroom soup**

¼ **cup sherry**

¼ **cup water**

1. In large bowl, combine ground beef, bread crumbs, minced onion, salt, pepper, nutmeg and beaten egg. Mix very well; shape into 24 meatballs, each about 1 inch in diameter.

2. Melt butter or margarine in large skillet over medium heat; add meatballs a few at a time and brown on all sides. Remove meatballs as browned and set aside. Drain surplus fat from skillet.

3. Stir mushroom soup, sherry and water into skillet; mix well to blend flavors. Bring sauce to simmering point over low heat; gently add meatballs. Simmer, covered, for 10 minutes.

FRIDAY NIGHT DINNER

Black Bean Soup with Onion
Garnish

Stuffed Peppers

Hearts of Lettuce with
Lemon Mayonnaise

Apple Granola

Serves 4.

WORK PLAN: Prepare Stuffed Peppers (see recipe below). Prepare dessert by dividing one 20-ounce can apple pie filling among four 10-ounce custard cups; top each with 2 tablespoons granola and dot with 1 tablespoon butter or margarine. Bake beside Stuffed Peppers for 20 minutes. Meanwhile, cut 4 heads Bibb or small heads Boston lettuce into fourths; arrange 4 sections on each of 4 salad plates. Top each with a little of ½ cup mayonnaise mixed with 2 tablespoons lemon juice and 1 teaspoon grated lemon rind. Heat one 11-ounce can black bean soup according to label directions; garnish with finely chopped onion.

Stuffed Peppers

4 medium-size green peppers

½ pound ground beef

1 cup quick-cooking rice

½ cup grated Cheddar cheese

two 6-ounce cans spiced tomato sauce

¼ cup water

1 tablespoon instant minced onion

½ teaspoon salt

1. Remove tops, seeds and membranes from green peppers; cook peppers, covered, in boiling salted water for 5 minutes. Drain well.

2. Brown ground beef in medium skillet over low heat for 3 to 4 minutes, stirring constantly to break meat into small pieces. Drain surplus fat from skillet.

3. Blend rice, grated cheese, 1 can of tomato sauce, the water, minced onion and salt into beef in skillet; stir to mix well. Fill peppers with beef mixture.

4. Place peppers in lightly greased, deep 1½-quart casserole. Bake, covered, at 375° F for 25 to 30 minutes. Heat remaining can of tomato sauce to serve with peppers.

GALA MEXICAN MENU

Gazpacho

Picadillo

Taco Chips

Artichokes with Pimientos

Marguerita Pie

Serves 4.

WORK PLAN: Prepare Marguerita Pie (see recipe below). Make Picadillo (see recipe below), and serve with taco chips. To make Gazpacho, combine 4 cups spicy tomato juice, ¼ cup olive oil and 2 cloves garlic, crushed, and chill in freezer; pour into 4 individual soup bowls just before serving. Serve with 1 cup each croutons, chopped tomatoes, chopped onion and chopped green pepper, placed in separate bowls, to be added to soup as desired. Heat two 8½-ounce cans artichoke hearts according to label directions; stir in one 4-ounce jar pimientos, drained and chopped. *Shown on page 69.*

Marguerita Pie

one 11-ounce package no-bake lemon pie mix

¼ cup tequila

¼ cup Triple Sec liqueur

½ teaspoon salt

½ cup heavy cream

lemon slices

1. Prepare pie shell, using ingredients in package and following label directions.

2. Prepare filling, substituting tequila and Triple Sec for ½ cup cold water and adding ½ teaspoon salt. Pour into pie shell; chill.

3. Just before serving, use electric mixer at high speed to beat heavy cream in medium bowl until stiff. Swirl over pie and decorate with lemon slices.

NOTE: Substitute ½ cup orange juice for tequila and Triple Sec if desired.

Picadillo

1 tablespoon vegetable oil
½ cup chopped onion
1 pound ground round beef
one 8-ounce can Spanish-style tomato sauce
1 tablespoon chili powder
1 tablespoon vinegar
1 teaspoon sugar
1 teaspoon cinnamon
½ teaspoon salt
1 cup slivered blanched almonds
1 cup grated Monterey Jack or mozzarella cheese

1. Heat oil in large skillet over medium heat; add onion and sauté until tender, about 3 to 4 minutes, stirring constantly.

2. Add ground beef; cook until all pink color disappears, stirring constantly to break meat into small pieces. Stir in tomato sauce, chili powder, vinegar, sugar, cinnamon and salt. Blend well.

3. Reduce heat to low and simmer, covered, for 20 minutes. Stir in almonds. Sprinkle with grated cheese, re-cover and cook just long enough to melt cheese.

THE KIDS' CHOICE

Minestrone

Meat Crust Pizza

Celery, Fennel and Corn Salad

Caramel Baked Apples

Serves 4.

WORK PLAN: Prepare dessert by coring 4 apples and setting in individual baking dishes. Pierce skins and fill center of each with mixture of 2 caramel candies, 1 teaspoon slivered almonds and ¼ teaspoon cinnamon; top with 1 tablespoon butter or margarine. Bake at 425° F for 40 minutes. Make Meat Crust Pizza (see recipe below) and bake along with apples. Make salad by combining 1 cup thinly sliced celery, 1 cup thinly sliced fennel, one 12-ounce can corn niblets, drained, and ½ cup Italian-style dressing; chill. Heat one 10½-ounce can minestrone soup according to label directions.

Meat Crust Pizza

1½ pounds ground beef
¼ cup soda cracker crumbs
1 tablespoon instant minced onion
½ teaspoon salt
¼ teaspoon garlic powder
one 8-ounce can tomato sauce
1 cup shredded mozzarella cheese
¼ cup grated Parmesan cheese
¾ teaspoon oregano

1. In large bowl, combine ground beef, cracker crumbs, minced onion, salt and garlic powder; mix well.

2. Place mixture on jelly roll pan (the sides of the pan will retain the meat juices). Press meat into a flat, round cake about 10 inches in diameter; shape ½-inch rim to keep sauce in place.

3. Pour tomato sauce evenly over meat. In small bowl, combine mozzarella and Parmesan cheese with oregano; sprinkle over sauce.

4. Bake pizza at 425° F for 20 to 25 minutes, until meat is cooked and sauce and cheese bubble. Let stand for 3 to 4 minutes before serving.

**SOUPER
SUPPER**

Beef and Beet Soup

Parslied Potatoes
Green Bean Salad

Fruit and Cream Ambrosia

Serves 4.

WORK PLAN: For dessert, prepare one 3¾-ounce package instant coconut cream pudding and pie filling according to label directions; fold in ½ cup heavy cream, stiffly beaten, one 11-ounce can mandarin oranges, well drained, and ½ cup chopped walnuts. Divide among 4 dessert dishes; chill. Peel 1 pound of potatoes and cut into walnut-size pieces; boil potatoes in salted water until tender, about 10 to 15 minutes. Drain, then toss with ¼ cup chopped parsley. Prepare salad by draining two 15-ounce cans whole green beans; toss beans with ½ cup garlic salad dressing and chill. Make Beef and Beet Soup (see recipe below).

Beef and Beet Soup

two 16-ounce cans julienne beets

one 10½-ounce can beef broth

½ cup thin onion rings

2 tablespoons brown sugar

¼ teaspoon ground allspice

1½ cups julienne strips cooked beef or tongue

¼ cup lemon juice

1 cup diced, seeded, pared cucumber

1 cup sour cream

1. In large saucepan, combine undrained beets, beef broth, onion rings, brown sugar and allspice. Cover and simmer over low heat for 5 minutes or until onions are tender.

2. Add julienne strips beef or tongue; heat 3 to 4 minutes longer. Stir in lemon juice; heat 1 minute longer but do not boil.

3. Divide soup among 4 soup bowls; serve diced cucumber and sour cream alongside.

TimeSaving Tip: Like the food processor, the microwave oven shaves down preparation time for a full-course meal to minutes. Each microwave model is different, so be sure to read menus and recipes with your make in mind. It's a good idea to arrest the cooking process a minute short of the recommended minimum time —it's easy to add cooking time and impossible to subtract it; overcooking can happen very quickly when a microwave oven is involved. Some microwaves have only a "high" setting, but they can be adjusted by using only a percentage of their full power, as specified in the microwave recipes that appear in this book.

**WEEKEND
FOOTBALL
SUPPER**

Tomato-Sherry Soup

Stuffed Acorn Squash

Skillet Mushroom and Corn
Casserole

Cranberry Snow

Serves 4.

WORK PLAN: Microwave squash until tender (see recipe below). Meanwhile, make dessert: Divide one 16-ounce can cranberry sauce among 4 dessert dishes; top with one 3¾-ounce package instant vanilla pudding and pie filling made according to label directions. Sprinkle each with 1 tablespoon toasted coconut; chill. To prepare vegetables, melt ¼ cup butter or margarine in large skillet over medium heat; add 4 cups thinly sliced mushrooms and sauté until tender. Add one 16-ounce polybag frozen whole kernel corn, ¼ cup dry white wine, 1½ teaspoons salt and ¼ teaspoon pepper; simmer, covered, until corn is tender. Add stuffing to acorn squash and reheat (see recipe below). Blend one 10¾-ounce can tomato soup with ½ cup water and ¼ cup dry sherry; divide among 4 soup cups and microwave on high setting for 1 minute while squash is standing at room temperature.

Stuffed Acorn Squash

2 **large acorn squash**

4 **slices bacon, cut into
½-inch pieces**

¼ **cup chopped onion**

1 **pound ground round beef**

1 **clove garlic, crushed**

½ **cup soda cracker crumbs**

1 **tablespoon Worcestershire
sauce**

¼ **teaspoon pepper**

¼ **cup ketchup**

1. Wash acorn squash; wipe dry. Pierce in several places with fork. Place two thicknesses of paper towels on floor of microwave oven; set squash on towels. Microwave on high setting for 12 to 14 minutes or until soft to the touch.

2. Let squash cool for 5 minutes. Cut lengthwise in half and scoop out seeds. Place squash halves in 12 x 7 x 2-inch glass baking dish; set aside.

3. Place bacon pieces in medium-size glass bowl; microwave on high setting for 2 minutes. Remove bacon from bowl with slotted spoon; set aside. Stir onion into bacon fat; microwave on high setting for 2 minutes.

4. Stir in ground beef; microwave on high setting for 4 minutes, stirring with fork to break meat into small pieces halfway through cooking process.

5. Add garlic, cracker crumbs, Worcestershire sauce and pepper. Divide mixture among 4 squash shells; spread each with 1 tablespoon ketchup. Microwave on high setting for 4 minutes. Let stand at room temperature for 2 minutes before serving.

DINNER WITH DASH

Veal Paprika

Noodles and Poppy Seeds
Sautéed Mushrooms

Cucumber Salad

Apple Pie Tarts

Serves 4.

WORK PLAN: First prepare dessert by baking one 11½-ounce package frozen apple pie tarts according to label directions. Next, prepare salad: Using vegetable parer, thinly slice 3 pared cucumbers; toss with ½ cup white vinegar, 2 tablespoons sugar, 1 teaspoon salt and ¼ teaspoon pepper; chill, and drain before serving. Cook one 16-ounce package noodles according to label directions. Toss with 2 tablespoons poppy seeds; keep warm while making Veal Paprika (see recipe below). Melt ¼ cup butter or margarine in medium skillet over medium heat; add 4 cups sliced mushrooms, 2 tablespoons lemon juice and ¼ teaspoon pepper and sauté for about 10 minutes, stirring occasionally.

Veal Paprika

4 veal cutlets

3 tablespoons butter or margarine

1 clove garlic, crushed

1 tablespoon paprika

½ teaspoon salt

½ cup chicken broth

1 cup sour cream

¼ cup chopped parsley

1. Wipe veal with damp paper towels. Place each cutlet between two sheets of waxed paper; using wooden mallet or rolling pin, pound to ¼-inch thickness (or have your butcher do this). Cut veal into 1-inch strips.

2. Melt butter or margarine in large skillet over medium heat; add veal and brown, about 2 minutes per side.

3. Add garlic; cook 1 minute longer, stirring constantly. Stir in paprika, salt and chicken broth. Reduce heat to low and simmer, covered, for 10 minutes.

4. Stir in sour cream; heat gently for 4 minutes (do not boil). Sprinkle with parsley.

ITALIAN FOOD PRONTO

Antipasto

Veal Piccata

Spinach Noodles
Buttery Herbed Tomatoes

Cheesecake

Serves 4.

WORK PLAN: To prepare dessert, thaw one 17-ounce packaged frozen cheesecake at room temperature. For antipasto, arrange 2 or 3 slices salami, 1 slice of provolone cheese cut into fingers, some black and green olives, and 2 or 3 spicy red and green peppers on each of 4 lettuce-lined salad plates. Dress with oil and vinegar and chill. Wash 1 pound cherry tomatoes and cut them in half. Melt 2 tablespoons butter or margarine in large skillet over medium heat; add halved tomatoes and sauté along with 1 teaspoon each salt, oregano and basil until tomatoes are tender. Make Veal Piccata (see recipe below). Meanwhile, cook one 16-ounce package spinach noodles according to label directions.

Veal Piccata

4 veal cutlets

¼ cup flour

½ teaspoon salt

¼ teaspoon pepper

¼ cup butter or margarine

¼ cup dry white wine

1 tablespoon lemon juice

2 tablespoons chopped parsley

1. Wipe veal cutlets with damp paper towels. Place each cutlet between two sheets of waxed paper; using wooden mallet or rolling pin, pound very thin (or have your butcher do this).

2. Mix together flour, salt and pepper on a plate. Dip cutlets in flour mixture to coat both sides. Melt butter or margarine in large skillet over medium heat; add veal and sauté to brown, 2 minutes per side. Remove veal to heated serving platter; keep warm.

3. Reduce heat to low. Add wine to skillet and heat for 2 minutes, stirring constantly to blend into pan drippings. Add lemon juice and heat 1 minute longer. Pour sauce over meat; sprinkle with parsley.

HARVEST HELPINGS

Pork Chops and Apples

Sautéed Squash
Celery Lima Beans

Date Nut Cake with Ice Cream

Serves 4.

WORK PLAN: Prepare one 15-ounce package date nut snack cake mix according to label directions; serve for dessert with ice cream on the side. Make Pork Chops and Apples (see recipe below). Meanwhile, melt 2 tablespoons butter or margarine in medium skillet over medium heat; add two 10-ounce packages frozen yellow squash slices and sauté until tender. Prepare one 16-ounce polybag frozen baby lima beans according to label directions; toss with ½ cup sour cream and ¼ cup chopped celery leaves.

Pork Chops and Apples

4 pork loin chops, 1 inch thick

2 tablespoons butter or margarine

1 cup chopped tart cooking apple

¼ cup brown sugar, firmly packed

½ teaspoon cinnamon

4 lemon slices

1. Wipe pork chops with damp paper towels. Melt butter or margarine in large skillet over medium heat; add pork chops and brown, about 2 minutes per side.

2. Place ¼ cup chopped apple on top of each pork chop. Reduce heat to low and cook, covered, for 20 minutes or until apple is tender.

3. Mix brown sugar and cinnamon and sprinkle over pork chops. Top each with lemon slice. Cover skillet again; cook 5 minutes longer or until sugar is melted.

**LEAF-RAKERS'
SPECIAL**

Lemony Tomato Soup

**Stuffed Pork Chops with
Mushroom Gravy**

Dilled Potatoes
Mixed Vegetables

Pear and Blue Cheese Platter

Serves 4.

WORK PLAN: Arrange 4 ripe pears and ¾ pound blue cheese, cut into wedges, on serving platter. Chill; let stand at room temperature for 30 minutes before serving for dessert. Make Stuffed Pork Chops with Mushroom Gravy (see recipe below). Prepare 1 pound of potatoes by peeling them and cutting them into ½-inch slices; cook in boiling salted water for 15 minutes, then drain and toss with 2 tablespoons butter or margarine and 2 tablespoons snipped fresh dill or 2 teaspoons dried dill. Prepare one 16-ounce polybag frozen mixed vegetables according to label directions. Finally, heat one 10¾-ounce can tomato soup with 1 cup water and 2 tablespoons lemon juice; serve with crisp croutons.

Stuffed Pork Chops with Mushroom Gravy

4 pork double loin chops

**2 slices white bread,
    quartered**

**one 3-ounce jar whole
    mushrooms, drained**

1 clove garlic, peeled

1 teaspoon salt

1 teaspoon rosemary

1 egg

⅓ cup vegetable oil

**one ¾-ounce package
    mushroom gravy mix**

¾ cup beef broth

**2 tablespoons chopped
    parsley**

1. Wipe pork chops well with damp paper towels; set chops aside.

2. With steel slicing blade in place in food processor, place bread, drained mushrooms, garlic, salt and rosemary in food processor bowl. Process until finely chopped, about 10 seconds.

3. Add egg to food processor bowl; process just long enough to mix well, about 3 to 4 seconds. Fill pork chop pockets with mixture. Secure slit of each pocket with toothpicks.

4. Heat oil in large skillet over medium heat; add chops and brown, about 3 minutes per side. Reduce heat to low and cook 20 to 25 minutes longer, turning once. Remove chops to heated serving platter; keep warm.

5. Pour all but 1 tablespoon drippings from skillet; stir mushroom gravy mix into drippings in skillet. Add beef broth and bring to boiling point over medium heat; simmer for 1 minute. Pour gravy over chops; sprinkle with parsley.

HOMECOMING FEAST

Speedy Pork with Raisin Sauce

Butternut Squash
Green Beans with Walnuts

Corn Bread Squares

Hot Fruit Cocktail with Butterscotch Sauce

Serves 4.

WORK PLAN: Prepare one 10-ounce package corn bread mix according to label directions. Place fruit cocktail from one 20-ounce can in 1-quart casserole; cover and heat in oven with the baking corn bread. Cook two 10-ounce packages frozen butternut squash according to label directions; beat in 2 tablespoons butter or margarine and keep warm. Heat green beans from one 15-ounce can; drain, then toss with 2 tablespoons butter or margarine and 2 tablespoons chopped walnuts. Keep beans warm while preparing Speedy Pork with Raisin Sauce (see recipe below). Heat two 5-ounce individual-size cans butterscotch pudding with ½ cup cream; stir in ½ teaspoon cinnamon and serve over hot fruit cocktail.

Speedy Pork with Raisin Sauce

one 12-ounce can processed pork meat

3 tablespoons brown sugar

2 teaspoons cornstarch

¼ teaspoon dry mustard

½ cup unsweetened apple juice

1 tablespoon lemon juice

½ cup golden raisins

¼ teaspoon cinnamon

⅛ teaspoon ginger

1. Remove pork meat from can (this is best done if chilled ahead of time); cut meat into 4 slices. Sauté slices on both sides in large skillet over medium heat until crisp and golden.

2. Meanwhile, blend sugar, cornstarch and dry mustard in small saucepan. Add apple juice and lemon juice, stirring to keep mixture smooth; add raisins, cinnamon and ginger.

3. Bring to boiling point over medium heat, stirring constantly. Reduce heat to low and simmer, covered, for 5 minutes to develop flavors. Place pork slices on serving platter; spoon sauce over meat.

SWEET AUTUMN FARE

Honey-Glazed Ham Steak

Candied Sweet Potatoes

Brussels Sprouts Parmesan

Baked Peaches with Nut Stuffing

Serves 4.

WORK PLAN: Preheat oven to 400° F. Prepare Honey-Glazed Ham Steak, Candied Sweet Potatoes and Baked Peaches with Nut Stuffing (see recipes below). Reduce oven heat to 350° F; place all three dishes in oven at once. Prepare two 10-ounce packages frozen Brussels sprouts according to label directions; drain, then toss with 2 tablespoons each butter or margarine and Parmesan cheese.

Honey-Glazed Ham Steak

2-pound ham steak, ¾ inch thick

¼ cup honey

1 tablespoon prepared spicy mustard

1 teaspoon grated lemon rind

¼ teaspoon ground cloves

1. Wipe ham steak with damp paper towels; place ham in shallow baking dish.

2. In small bowl, blend honey, mustard, lemon rind and cloves. Spread over ham steak. Bake at 350° F for 25 minutes, basting occasionally with pan juices.

Candied Sweet Potatoes

one 18-ounce can sweet
  potatoes, drained

¾ cup brown sugar, firmly
  packed

1 tablespoon lemon juice

½ teaspoon cinnamon

¼ teaspoon nutmeg

2 tablespoons butter or
  margarine

1. Place drained sweet potatoes in lightly greased, shallow 1-quart casserole.

2. In small bowl, mix together brown sugar, lemon juice, cinnamon and nutmeg; sprinkle over sweet potatoes. Dot with butter or margarine. Bake at 350° F for 25 minutes or until hot and bubbling.

Baked Peaches with Nut Stuffing

one 16-ounce can cling
  peach halves

¾ cup nut-flavored cookie
  crumbs

8 pecan halves

½ cup sherry

¼ teaspoon ginger

pouring cream or whipped
  cream (optional)

1. Drain peach halves, reserving ¼ cup syrup. Place peach halves cut side up in lightly greased 8 x 8 x 2-inch baking dish.

2. In small bowl, mix together cookie crumbs and reserved peach syrup; fill cavities of peach halves with mixture. Top each with a pecan half.

3. Blend together sherry and ginger; pour around peaches. Bake at 350° F for 25 minutes. Serve with pouring cream or stiffly beaten heavy cream if desired.

FALL COLORS MENU

Ginger Turnips and Ham

Sautéed Sweet Potato Crisps
Chicory Salad

Pear and Ricotta Dessert

Serves 4.

WORK PLAN: Prepare dessert: Blend 1 cup ricotta or small curd cottage cheese with ½ cup each sugar, golden raisins and chopped toasted slivered almonds. Drain one 20-ounce can pear halves; place 2 pear halves in each of 4 dessert dishes with ½ cup filling between halves. Pour one-fourth of an 8-ounce jar chocolate sauce over each; chill. To prepare salad, chill 4 cups bite-size pieces chicory; toss with ½ cup red wine vinegar and oil salad dressing just before serving. Peel 1 pound sweet potatoes and cut potatoes into ¼-inch slices. Heat 2 tablespoons oil in large skillet; add potatoes and stir-fry until crisp-tender. Keep potatoes warm while making Ginger Turnips and Ham (see recipe below).

Ginger Turnips and Ham

2 cups julienne strips
yellow turnip

1 pound precooked ham

¼ cup vegetable oil

1 tablespoon soy sauce

1 teaspoon sugar

½ teaspoon ginger

½ pound spinach leaves,
stems removed, or 2 cups
bite-size pieces Swiss
chard

1. Add turnip strips to 1 inch of boiling water in medium saucepan; reduce heat to low and simmer until tender, about 15 minutes. Drain well. Meanwhile, cut ham into julienne strips.

2. Heat oil in large skillet, electric skillet or wok; add ham and turnip strips and stir-fry until lightly browned, about 1 minute.

3. Stir in soy sauce, sugar and ginger. Add washed spinach leaves or Swiss chard. Stir-fry until greens are slightly wilted.

**FOOD FOR
NIPPY WEATHER**

Hot-Sour Soup

Ham Patties Cordon Bleu

Pan-Fried Tomatoes
Spicy Creamed Spinach

Jelly Roll and Ice Cream

Serves 4.

WORK PLAN: Prepare soup by heating one 10½-ounce can beef bouillon with 1 cup water, 2 tablespoons red wine vinegar, 1 tablespoon soy sauce and 2 to 3 drops hot pepper sauce; keep warm. Prepare spinach by cooking two 10-ounce packages frozen chopped spinach according to label directions; drain. Stir in ¼ cup cream and ½ teaspoon nutmeg; keep warm. Prepare dessert by cutting four ½-inch slices from store-bought jelly roll; set on individual dessert platters. Top each with large scoop of ice cream from 1½ pints; freeze. Prepare Ham Patties Cordon Bleu (see recipe below); keep warm. Place 4 tomato halves cut side down in skillet containing drippings from patties; fry for 3 to 4 minutes.

Ham Patties Cordon Bleu

one 16-ounce can ham
patties

4 slices Swiss cheese

1 cup all-purpose flour

1 egg

1 tablespoon water

1½ cups dry unseasoned
bread crumbs

¼ cup butter or margarine

½ cup chopped parsley

lemon wedges

1. Remove ham patties from can and separate. For each portion, place a cheese slice between 2 ham patties, trimming cheese to fit. Dip patties into flour to coat; dust off surplus.

2. Beat together egg and water; pour onto plate. Place bread crumbs on second plate. Dip patties in egg mixture to coat; drain slightly, then dip into breadcrumbs, pressing firmly to coat.

3. Melt butter or margarine in large skillet over medium heat; add patties and brown, about 2 to 3 minutes per side, turning carefully with wide spatula. Remove from skillet and place on serving platter; sprinkle with parsley and garnish with lemon wedges.

SUPPER AT HEARTHSIDE

Canadian Bacon with Spicy Apricots

Hot Dinner Rolls

Brussels Sprouts

Three Bean Salad

Applesauce and Brownies

Serves 4.

WORK PLAN: Prepare salad by mixing together one 15-ounce can each green beans, red kidney beans and chick peas, drained, with ½ cup garlic dressing; chill. Prepare one 15½-ounce package brownie mix according to label directions; bake at 350° F along with Canadian Bacon with Spicy Apricots (see recipe below). Prepare two 10-ounce packages frozen Brussels sprouts according to label directions; keep warm. Wrap 4 dinner rolls in foil and place in oven to heat. Spoon ¾ cup applesauce from one 32-ounce jar into each of 4 serving dishes; chill until ready to serve with warm brownie squares.

Canadian Bacon with Spicy Apricots

1-pound piece Canadian bacon

¼ cup apricot or peach preserves

one 6-ounce can apricot halves, drained

2 tablespoons brown sugar

½ teaspoon cinnamon

1. Slice Canadian bacon into 8 equal sections, cutting three-quarters of the way through bacon so slices are still attached at base of meat.

2. Place meat in small casserole or baking dish; spoon 1½ teaspoons preserves between each slice. Arrange apricots cut side up around bacon; sprinkle fruit with mixture of brown sugar and cinnamon. Bake at 350° F for 20 minutes or until meat is heated through.

HUNTERS' HOT MEAL

Celery Soup

Bratwurst and Home-Fried Potatoes

Buttered Caraway Cabbage Wedges

Sweet Apple Rings

Serves 4.

WORK PLAN: Prepare one 10¾-ounce can cream of celery soup according to label directions; keep warm. Cut 1 small cabbage into 4 wedges; place on wire rack in large saucepan containing ½ cup salted water. Bring to simmering point and steam for about 15 minutes, until tender. Keep warm, and serve drizzled with melted butter and sprinkled with caraway seeds. Prepare Bratwurst and Home-Fried Potatoes (see recipe below). Make dessert by coring 4 large sweet apples; cut apples into ½-inch slices. Melt ¼ cup butter or margarine in large skillet over medium heat; add apple slices and fry until tender, sprinkling with ⅓ cup firmly packed brown sugar.

Bratwurst and Home-Fried Potatoes

4 large or 8 small bratwurst

2 slices bacon, cut up

4 medium potatoes, peeled and coarsely grated

2 tablespoons chopped onion

2 tablespoons chopped green pepper

½ teaspoon salt

¼ teaspoon pepper

1. Prick bratwurst very well with fork; place in large saucepan in 2 inches of cold water. Bring to boiling point over medium heat. Reduce heat to low and simmer, covered, for 6 to 8 minutes.

2. Meanwhile, fry bacon pieces in large skillet over medium heat until fat melts and coats bottom of skillet. Add potatoes, onion, green pepper, salt and pepper to skillet; mix well. Cook mixture for 8 minutes or until golden crust is formed. Slide potato mixture onto platter, then invert back into pan. Arrange bratwurst around edge.

3. Cook about 6 to 8 minutes longer, until potatoes are crusty and brown on bottom; turn bratwurst every 2 to 3 minutes.

**RUSTIC
FALL MENU**

Vegetable Soup

Sausage Ring with Hot Bean Salad

Hot Pumpernickel Bread

Green Grapes with Yogurt and Brown Sugar

Serves 4.

WORK PLAN: Prepare dessert by washing and drying 1½ pounds green seedless grapes; place in dessert bowl and mix with one 16-ounce container low-fat unflavored yogurt. Sprinkle with ¼ cup brown sugar; chill. Heat one 10½-ounce can vegetable soup according to label directions; keep warm. Prepare Sausage Ring with Hot Bean Salad (see recipe below). Slice pumpernickel loaf; reassemble into loaf, wrap in foil and warm in oven beside Sausage Ring.

Sausage Ring with Hot Bean Salad

1½- to 2-pound kielbasa or garlic sausage ring

one 16-ounce can red kidney beans, drained

one 16-ounce can navy beans, drained

¼ cup finely chopped onion

¼ cup chopped parsley

⅓ cup vegetable oil

¼ cup red wine vinegar

1 teaspoon salt

½ teaspoon pepper

onion rings (optional)

1. Pierce sausage well with fork; place in large saucepan and cover with water. Bring to boiling point over medium heat; reduce heat to low and simmer for 5 minutes. Remove sausage from pan.

2. Meanwhile, blend drained kidney beans and navy beans, onion, parsley, oil, vinegar, salt and pepper in large bowl. Place in 9-inch pie plate or shallow round baking dish.

3. Using sharp knife, make diagonal cuts every few inches around outer edge of sausage; place sausage on top of beans. Bake at 450° F for 10 to 15 minutes or until sausage is brown and beans are piping hot. Garnish with raw onion rings if desired.

LAST-MINUTE HIGHLAND SUPPER

Baked Scotch Eggs

Baked Tomatoes
Spinach Casserole

Crusty Bread

Pears à l'Orange

Serves 4.

WORK PLAN: Prepare Baked Scotch Eggs (see recipe below). Cut 2 large tomatoes in half. Using tip of sharp knife, cut center flesh deeply two or three times; sprinkle with salt and pepper and place in baking dish around Scotch Eggs as they are cooking. Thaw two 10-ounce packages chopped spinach under hot running water. Drain dry; place in lightly greased casserole and mix with ½ cup sour cream, 1 teaspoon salt, ¼ teaspoon pepper and ¼ teaspoon nutmeg. Place casserole in oven beside Scotch Eggs for 20 to 25 minutes. Wrap loaf of crusty bread in foil; heat in oven for 15 minutes. Divide one 20-ounce can pear halves among 4 dessert dishes; chill. In electric blender, puree one 11-ounce can mandarin oranges; serve with pears. *Shown on page 70.*

Baked Scotch Eggs

4 eggs

1 pound mildly seasoned bulk sausage meat

¾ cup soda cracker crumbs

¼ cup chopped parsley

1 tablespoon instant minced onion

1 tablespoon grated Parmesan cheese

½ teaspoon oregano

1. Pierce each egg at blunt end with needle; place in medium saucepan and cover with cold water. Bring to boiling point; reduce heat and simmer, covered, for 5 minutes. Plunge immediately into cold water. Crack shells; keep in water until cold enough to peel off shells. Eggs will be slightly soft inside.

2. In large bowl, mix together sausage meat, cracker crumbs, parsley, minced onion, grated cheese and oregano. Divide mixture into 4 equal parts.

3. On lightly floured board, pat each portion out into a 4- to 5-inch circle; gently mold a portion around each egg. Place in baking pan; bake at 400° F for 30 minutes.

○ *TimeSaving Tip:* Having dried herbs and aromatic ingredients such as instant minced onions on hand adds up to time-saving convenience. Use only half as much of a dried herb as you would a fresh one. For best flavor, buy dried herbs only in small quantities and store them in airtight containers in a cool dark place. Also, it's better to have six or eight of your favorite herbs in stock than to keep 20 herbs on hand that you seldom use—they'll lose their flavor before you've had a chance to cook with them.

**HALLOWEEN
TREAT**

Golden Mushroom Soup

Frank and Cabbage Sauté

Herb-Seasoned Rice

Hot Butterscotch Sundaes

Serves 4.

WORK PLAN: Prepare dessert by dividing 1½ pints vanilla ice cream among 4 individual dessert dishes; freeze. Prepare Hot Butterscotch Sauce (see recipe below). Heat one 10¾-ounce can golden mushroom soup according to label directions; keep warm. Prepare one 6-ounce package herb-seasoned rice mix according to label directions; keep warm. Prepare Frank and Cabbage Sauté (see recipe below).

Hot Butterscotch Sauce

¾ cup brown sugar, firmly packed

¼ cup light corn syrup

1 tablespoon butter or margarine

⅓ cup evaporated milk

½ teaspoon vanilla extract

1. In small saucepan, blend brown sugar, corn syrup and butter or margarine. Bring to boiling point over low heat, stirring constantly; boil for 2 minutes.

2. Stir in evaporated milk and vanilla extract; keep warm and serve over ice cream.

Makes 1⅓ cups.

Frank and Cabbage Sauté

2 tablespoons butter or margarine

1 small head cabbage, shredded

¼ cup chopped onion

½ teaspoon salt

¼ teaspoon pepper

¼ teaspoon thyme

1 cup tomato juice

8 frankfurters, cut into ½-inch diagonal slices

1. Melt butter or margarine in large skillet over medium heat; add cabbage and onion and sauté for 2 minutes, stirring constantly.

2. Add salt, pepper, thyme and tomato juice; stir to mix well. Gently stir in frankfurter slices. Reduce heat to low and simmer, covered, for 10 minutes, until franks are hot and cabbage is crisp-tender.

BEFORE-THE-MOVIES SUPPER

Quick-Fry Chicken and Gravy

Hot Biscuits
Succotash

Ice Cream Cake

Serves 4.

WORK PLAN: Prepare Quick-Fry Chicken and Gravy (see recipe below). Using 2 cups packaged biscuit mix, make biscuits according to label directions. Cook one 16-ounce polybag frozen succotash according to label directions. To prepare dessert, fill 4 individual sponge cake dessert shells with scoops from 1½ pints strawberry ice cream; garnish with some partially thawed strawberry slices from one 12-ounce package. Top with shredded coconut and freeze.

Quick-Fry Chicken and Gravy

2½- to 3-pound broiler-fryer chicken, cut into serving pieces

1 cup flour

1 teaspoon salt

¼ teaspoon pepper

¼ teaspoon paprika

1 cup vegetable oil

one 10¾-ounce can cream of chicken soup

¾ cup milk

2 tablespoons chopped parsley

½ teaspoon grated lemon rind

1. Wash chicken pieces under cold running water; pat dry with paper towels. In large, clean brown paper or plastic bag, combine flour, salt, pepper and paprika. Place chicken pieces two at a time in bag; shake to coat well.

2. Heat oil in large skillet over medium heat until surface of oil ripples and has a slight haze. Place chicken skin side down in hot oil to brown for about 5 minutes. Turn and fry other side 5 minutes. Reduce heat to low and continue to fry for 10 to 15 minutes, until chicken is crisp and tender, turning frequently. Drain chicken on paper towels. Place chicken on serving platter and keep warm.

3. Make pan gravy by pouring off all but 2 tablespoons oil from skillet. Blend soup into drippings in skillet; add milk, parsley and grated lemon rind. Bring to boiling point over medium heat, stirring constantly. Serve alongside chicken.

FIRST FROST DINNER

Onion-Paprika Chicken

Egg Noodles
Red Cabbage

Cucumber-Fennel Salad

Sweet Chestnut Sundaes

Serves 4.

WORK PLAN: To prepare dessert, drain one 12-ounce jar chestnuts in syrup; reserve juice and crumble chestnuts. Divide all but 2 tablespoons chestnuts among 4 dessert glasses; divide 1½ pints vanilla ice cream among glasses. Pour reserved chestnut syrup over ice cream and sprinkle with reserved chestnuts; freeze. Make salad by tossing 3 cups pared and sliced cucumbers and 1 cup sliced fennel with ½ cup sour cream and 1 teaspoon onion salt; divide among 4 salad plates and chill. Make Onion-Paprika Chicken (see recipe below). Meanwhile, prepare one 16-ounce package egg noodles according to label directions, and heat red cabbage from one 16-ounce jar until very hot.

Onion-Paprika Chicken

2½-pound broiler-fryer chicken, cut into serving pieces

¼ cup flour

2 tablespoons butter or margarine

one 10¾-ounce can cream of onion soup

⅓ cup dry red wine

⅓ cup water

1 tablespoon paprika

1. Wash chicken pieces under cold running water; pat dry with paper towels. Sprinkle chicken with flour, rubbing into all surfaces.

2. Melt butter or margarine in large skillet over medium heat; add chicken pieces and sauté, turning to brown all sides. Remove from skillet and set aside.

3. Add soup, wine, water and paprika to drippings in skillet; bring to boiling point, stirring constantly. Return chicken to skillet. Reduce heat to low and simmer, covered, for 20 minutes or until chicken is tender.

**SAVORY
SEPTEMBER MEAL**

Chicken Marengo

Buttered Rice and Artichoke Hearts

Rum Cake

Serves 4.

2½- to 3-pound broiler-fryer chicken, cut into serving pieces

½ cup flour

¼ cup vegetable oil

one 16-ounce jar whole white onions, drained

one 14½-ounce can stewed tomatoes

½ cup dry white wine

¼ teaspoon garlic powder

¼ teaspoon oregano

½ cup pitted black olives

one 4-ounce can mushroom pieces, drained

¼ cup chopped parsley

WORK PLAN: Prepare Chicken Marengo (see recipe below). Cook 1 cup long-grain rice according to label directions; toss with one 6-ounce jar artichoke hearts, drained and quartered, and 2 tablespoons butter or margarine. Keep warm. Cut one 9½-ounce pound cake into 4 horizontal slices; sprinkle each with 1 tablespoon rum or orange juice. Stiffly beat ¾ cup heavy cream with 2 tablespoons confectioners' sugar. Use to fill cake layers; chill.

Chicken Marengo

1. Wash chicken pieces under cold running water; pat dry with paper towels. Sprinkle chicken with flour, rubbing into all surfaces.

2. Heat oil in 2-quart heatproof casserole over medium heat; add chicken pieces and sauté for about 10 minutes, turning to brown all sides. Stir in drained onions, tomatoes, wine, garlic powder and oregano.

3. Cover and bake at 400° F for 25 minutes. Stir in olives and drained mushrooms. Cook 10 minutes longer. Sprinkle with parsley.

ALPINE REPAST

Swiss-Style Chicken

Spaetzle
Pan-Fried Mushrooms

Chocolate Fondue with
Fruits

Serves 4.

WORK PLAN: First combine 4 cups sliced mushrooms, ½ cup red wine, ¼ cup butter or margarine, 1½ teaspoons salt and ¼ teaspoon pepper in medium skillet. Cover and cook over low heat until mushrooms are tender, stirring occasionally; keep warm. To prepare dessert, blend two 5-ounce individual-size cans chocolate pudding, ½ cup heavy cream and ½ cup semisweet chocolate morsels in fondue pot over low heat; stir to melt chocolate. Keep warm and serve over canned heat source with chunks of apples, pears and strawberries for dipping with fondue forks. Prepare Swiss-Style Chicken (see recipe below). Meanwhile, prepare one 10-ounce package spaetzle mix according to label directions (or use one 8-ounce package macaroni shells cooked according to label directions).

Swiss-Style Chicken

4 chicken breast halves, skinned and boned

⅓ cup flour

¼ teaspoon pepper

2 tablespoons butter or margarine

one ⅞-ounce package brown gravy mix

¾ cup water

¼ cup dry red wine

2 slices Swiss cheese, cut in half

2 tablespoons chopped parsley

4 lemon wedges

1. Wash chicken breast halves under cold running water; pat dry with paper towels. Sprinkle both sides of chicken with mixture of flour and pepper; rub well into all surfaces.

2. Melt butter or margarine in large skillet over medium heat; add chicken and brown, 2 minutes per side. Reduce heat to low; continue to cook until chicken is tender, about 10 minutes longer.

3. Meanwhile, blend gravy mix, water and wine in small saucepan. Bring to boiling point over medium heat, stirring constantly.

4. When chicken breast halves are browned and tender, place half a cheese slice on top of each. Cover skillet for 2 minutes to melt cheese.

5. Place chicken breasts on serving platter and coat with a little gravy. Sprinkle with parsley and garnish with lemon wedges. Serve remaining gravy alongside.

SLAVIC FEAST FOR FALL

Sherried Asparagus Soup

Chicken Smetana

Kasha

Celery and Carrot Casserole

Grape and Peach Compote

Tea Biscuits

Serves 4.

WORK PLAN: In large dessert bowl, combine one 20-ounce can un-drained cling peach slices and one 8-ounce can green grapes, drained; chill, and serve with packaged tea biscuits. Prepare Celery and Carrot Casserole (see recipe below). Prepare kasha by cooking 1 cup buckwheat groats according to label directions. Make Chicken Smetana (see recipe below). Meanwhile, heat one 10¾-ounce can cream of asparagus soup with 1 cup chicken broth and ¼ cup dry sherry. *Shown on front cover.*

Carrot and Celery Casserole

4 stalks celery

4 medium carrots, peeled and cut into 3-inch pieces

1 medium onion, peeled and quartered

2 tablespoons butter or margarine

¼ cup beef broth

¼ cup red wine

½ teaspoon salt

½ teaspoon thyme

1. With steel slicing blade in place in food processor, place celery stalks in tube in processor lid. Slice celery by pressing down pusher. Slice carrots by placing cut side down in tube and pressing down pusher. Slice onion in same way.

2. Melt butter or margarine in large skillet over low heat; add celery, carrots and onion and sauté until onion is golden. Pour in beef broth and wine. Sprinkle with salt and thyme; stir to mix well.

3. Reduce heat to low and simmer, covered, for 10 minutes or until vegetables are tender, stirring occasionally.

Chicken Smetana

4 chicken breast halves, skinned and boned

1 teaspoon salt

¼ teaspoon pepper

¼ cup butter or margarine

1 pound mushrooms

1 large onion, sliced

1 cup sour cream

¼ cup dry white wine

lemon wedges

1. Wash chicken well under cold running water; pat dry with paper towels. Place each chicken breast half between two sheets of waxed paper; using wooden mallet or rolling pin, pound very thin (or have your butcher do this). Sprinkle each chicken breast half with a little salt and pepper.

2. Melt 2 tablespoons of the butter or margarine in large skillet over medium heat; add chicken breasts and sauté until tender, about 3 minutes per side. Remove to heated serving platter; keep warm.

3. With steel slicing blade in place in food processor, place mushrooms in tube in processor lid. Slice mushrooms by pressing down pusher. Set mushrooms aside.

4. With steel all-purpose blade in place in food processor, place onion in food processor bowl; chop finely by rapidly turning machine on and off for 15 seconds.

5. Melt remaining 2 tablespoons butter or margarine in same skillet over medium heat; add onion and sauté until tender, about 4 minutes, stirring constantly. Add mushrooms; cook 2 minutes longer.

6. Blend in sour cream and wine; heat to simmering point but do not boil. Pour sauce over chicken; serve with lemon wedges.

CHINESE
CHICKEN DINNER

Chicken with Peanuts

Brown Rice
Oriental Vegetables

Orange and Pineapple
Dessert

Serves 4.

WORK PLAN: Prepare Chicken with Peanuts (see recipe below). While chicken is marinating, make dessert by draining and combining juice from one 16-ounce can pineapple chunks and one 11-ounce can mandarin oranges; divide fruit among 4 dessert dishes and add ¼ cup juice to each. Chill. Prepare 1½ cups uncooked natural brown rice according to label directions. Cook one 10-ounce package frozen Japanese-style vegetables according to label directions, adding 2 cups shredded spinach as vegetables cook.

Chicken with Peanuts

1 pound chicken breasts, skinned and boned

1 tablespoon cornstarch

1 tablespoon dry sherry

1 egg white

¼ cup vegetable oil

1 cup salted peanuts

1. Wash chicken well under cold running water; pat dry with paper towels. Cut chicken into ¾-inch cubes. In medium bowl, blend cornstarch, sherry, and egg white. Stir in chicken to coat well; marinate at room temperature for 30 minutes.

2. Heat oil in large skillet, electric skillet or wok; remove chicken from marinade and stir-fry in hot oil until golden, about 1 minute.

3. Sprinkle peanuts over chicken; stir-fry 1 minute longer.

FIRST-CLASS
AUSTRIAN FEAST

Cream of Asparagus Soup

Viennese Chicken Cutlets

Golden Rice
Beans and Chestnuts
Almondine

Hearts of Lettuce with
Cucumber Dressing

Apple Dream

Serves 4.

WORK PLAN: To prepare salad, wash and dry 4 heads of Bibb or tiny heads of Boston lettuce; cut each head into quarters and put 4 pieces on each of 4 individual salad plates. Fill center with cucumber dressing and chill. Cook one 16-ounce polybag green beans according to label directions; toss with one 8-ounce can chestnuts, drained and sliced, ½ cup slivered almonds and ¼ cup butter or margarine. Keep vegetables warm. Cook 1 cup long-grain rice according to label directions, adding 1 tablespoon Dijon-style mustard. Meanwhile, prepare Viennese Chicken Cutlets (see recipe below) and heat one 10¾-ounce can cream of asparagus soup according to label directions. Prepare dessert by beating 1 cup heavy cream until stiff and folding it into one 16-ounce jar sweetened applesauce. Place in bowl and sprinkle with chopped or slivered nuts; serve immediately.

Viennese Chicken Cutlets

4 chicken breast halves,
skinned and boned

1 egg

1 tablespoon water

1 cup dry seasoned bread
crumbs

¼ cup butter or margarine

4 lemon wedges

1. Place each chicken breast half between two sheets of waxed paper; using wooden mallet or rolling pin, pound chicken breasts to ¼-inch thickness (or have your butcher do this).

2. Beat together egg and water; pour onto plate. Place bread crumbs on second plate. Dip chicken cutlets one at a time into egg mixture to coat both sides; drain slightly. Dip into bread crumbs, pressing crumbs firmly to coat both sides of cutlets.

3. Melt butter or margarine in large skillet over medium heat; add chicken cutlets and sauté until crisp, brown and tender, about 2 minutes per side. Place on platter; garnish with lemon wedges.

**HASTY
COOL-WEATHER
MEAL**

Tomato-Cucumber Salad
Drumsticks and Rice
Mixed Vegetable Casserole
Lemon-Ginger Desserts
Serves 4.

WORK PLAN: Prepare salad by dividing 2 thinly sliced tomatoes and 1 thinly sliced pared cucumber among 4 salad plates; top each portion with 3 to 4 thin onion slices. Spoon oil and vinegar dressing on each salad and chill. Prepare Drumsticks and Rice (see recipe below). Cook one 16-ounce polybag frozen mixed vegetables according to label directions; drain, and top with ¼ cup finely diced mozzarella cheese before serving. For dessert, prepare one 3¾-ounce package instant lemon pudding and divide pudding among 4 dessert glasses, layering with crushed gingersnaps.

Drumsticks and Rice

8 chicken drumsticks

¼ cup flour

2 tablespoons butter or
margarine

one 10¾-ounce can golden
mushroom soup

half of 2¾-ounce package
onion soup mix

2 cups water

1⅓ cups quick-cooking rice

1. Wash chicken under cold running water; pat dry with paper towels. In large, clean brown paper or plastic bag, shake drumsticks two at a time with flour to coat.

2. Melt butter or margarine in large skillet over medium heat; add drumsticks and sauté, turning to brown all sides. Reduce heat to low; cook, covered, for 15 minutes or until tender, turning occasionally. Remove chicken to heated serving platter; keep warm.

3. Using wire whisk, stir mushroom soup and onion soup mix into drippings in skillet. Slowly stir in water. Bring to boiling point over medium heat, stirring constantly. Stir in rice; remove from heat, cover and let stand for 5 minutes. Make rice border around the chicken drumsticks.

**ZIPPY
HOT AND COLD
SUPPER**

Hearty Onion Soup

Health Salad

Sliced Turkey and Chicken

Apple Pancakes

Serves 4.

WORK PLAN: Prepare Hearty Onion Soup (see recipe below). While soup is cooking, prepare Health Salad (see recipe below). Arrange ¾ pound each sliced cooked turkey and chicken on serving platter; cover and chill until serving time. Prepare Apple Pancakes for dessert (see recipe below).

Hearty Onion Soup

1 pound onions, peeled and halved

2 tablespoons butter or margarine

½ teaspoon sugar

two 10½-ounce cans beef broth

1½ cups water

½ cup red Burgundy wine

¼ teaspoon pepper

½ pound Swiss cheese

4 slices French or Italian bread, ½ inch thick

1. With steel slicing blade in place in food processor, place onions in tube in processor lid. Slice by pressing down pusher.

2. Melt butter or margarine in 4-quart saucepan over medium heat; add onions, sprinkle with sugar and sauté until golden brown, about 10 minutes, stirring occasionally. Add beef broth, water, wine and pepper; reduce heat to low and simmer, covered, for 30 minutes.

3. Preheat broiler.

4. With steel shredding blade in place in food processor, place cheese in tube in processor lid. Shred cheese by pressing down pusher. Set cheese aside. Toast bread; set aside. Divide soup among 4 heatproof bowls. Float a toasted bread slice in each; sprinkle with shredded cheese. Broil 3 inches from heat until cheese is melted and slightly browned.

Health Salad

1 small head romaine

2 medium carrots, peeled and cut into 3-inch pieces

2 stalks celery

1 small cucumber, pared and cut lengthwise in half

1 small onion, peeled and quartered

⅓ cup olive oil

2 tablespoons red wine vinegar

½ teaspoon salt

¼ teaspoon pepper

¼ teaspoon dry mustard

1. Wash lettuce; pat dry with paper towels. Break leaves into bite-size pieces; place in salad bowl.

2. With steel shredding blade in place in food processor, place carrots cut side down in tube in processor lid. Shred carrots by pressing down pusher. Process celery stalks the same way. Sprinkle carrots and celery over lettuce.

3. With steel slicing blade in place in food processor, place cucumber in tube in processor lid. Slice cucumber by pressing down pusher. Process onion the same way; add both to lettuce. Toss well; chill.

4. With steel all-purpose blade in place in food processor, place oil, vinegar, salt, pepper and dry mustard in food processor bowl; process for 4 seconds to mix well. Toss with salad just before serving.

Apple Pancakes

2 medium apples, peeled,
   cored and quartered
1 cup packaged pancake
   mix
1 tablespoon sugar
½ teaspoon cinnamon
1 egg
⅔ cup milk
2 tablespoons vegetable oil
½ teaspoon vanilla extract
confectioners' sugar
1½ cups applesauce

1. With steel shredding blade in place in food processor, place apple quarters in tube in processor lid. Shred apples by pressing down pusher.

2. Leaving shredded apples in food processor bowl, set steel all-purpose blade in place. Add pancake mix, sugar, cinnamon, egg, milk, oil and vanilla extract to processor bowl. Process just until blended, turning machine on and off for 3 seconds.

3. Fry pancakes on preheated griddle until golden on both sides. Serve warm, sprinkled with confectioners' sugar; serve applesauce alongside pancakes.

TimeSaving Tip: Apples make good side dishes and desserts for quick dinners because they can cook virtually untended while you prepare other parts of the meal. It's important to select the right kind of apple for cooking. Raw McIntosh apples are great for munching, but are too juicy for cooking. If you plan to bake apples, buy Rome Beauty, Delicious (both red and yellow), Granny Smith, Greening or Pippin. If you can find time to bake a pie, try Cortland or Jonathan apples. When you're shopping for apples, pick the ones that are the color they're supposed to be—uniform green for Granny Smith, unmottled yellow for Golden Delicious, etc.—and watch out for bruises and soft spots.

TURKEY DINNER ORIENTALE

Chilled Cranberry-Apple Juice

Turkey Chow Mein

Oriental Fruit Compote

Serves 4.

2 tablespoons vegetable oil

2 cups cubed cooked turkey, or 1 pound precooked turkey roll, cubed

½ cup chopped onion

½ cup chopped celery

one 10¾-ounce can golden mushroom soup

one 11¾-ounce can Chinese vegetables, rinsed and drained

1 tablespoon soy sauce

2 cups crisp chow mein noodles

WORK PLAN: Prepare juice: Divide 3 cups cranberry-apple juice among 4 glasses; garnish each with 2 or 3 thin unpeeled apple slices and chill. To prepare dessert, combine one 16-ounce can undrained lychees, one 11-ounce can mandarin oranges, drained, and one 8-ounce can pineapple chunks, drained, in large dessert bowl. Sprinkle with ½ cup slivered toasted almonds; chill. Prepare Turkey Chow Mein (see recipe below).

Turkey Chow Mein

1. Heat oil in large skillet over medium heat; add turkey, onion and celery and stir-fry for 2 minutes.

2. Reduce heat to low; blend in soup, Chinese vegetables and soy sauce. Cook until very hot, about 3 minutes, stirring constantly.

3. Meanwhile, warm chow mein noodles in 300° F oven. Serve turkey mixture over warm crisp noodles.

POST-THANKSGIVING PARTY

Turkey Crêpes

Savory Apples
Braised Carrots

Fruit Cocktail
Snack Cake

Serves 4.

WORK PLAN: To make dessert, prepare one 15-ounce snack cake mix according to label directions; divide one 16-ounce can fruit cocktail among 4 individual dessert glasses and chill. Heat pie-sliced apples from one 20-ounce can in medium saucepan; just before serving, drain apples and stir in 2 tablespoons butter or margarine and ½ teaspoon each grated lemon rind and cinnamon. Cook one 16-ounce polybag frozen baby carrots according to label directions; drain, and toss with 2 tablespoons butter or margarine and 2 tablespoons chopped parsley. Keep carrots warm while preparing Turkey Crêpes (see recipe below).

Turkey Crêpes

CREPES

1 cup packaged pancake mix

1½ cups water

2 eggs

2 tablespoons butter, margarine or vegetable shortening, melted

butter or margarine for frying

FILLING

1 tablespoon butter or margarine

2 tablespoons chopped onion

two 6¾-ounce cans turkey chunks

one 10¾-ounce can cream of chicken soup

¼ cup dry sherry

1 tablespoon lemon juice

1. To make crêpes, use wire whisk to combine pancake mix, water, eggs and melted shortening in large bowl; blend until smooth. Let stand in refrigerator for at least 1 hour.

2. For each crêpe, melt 1 teaspoon butter or margarine in 6- to 8-inch skillet over medium heat. Pour in 2 tablespoons batter; tilt skillet to coat bottom evenly with batter. Cook for 30 seconds or until edge begins to brown; turn with spatula and cook second side for 20 seconds. Continue until all batter is used.

3. Stack crêpes between layers of waxed paper. Wrap completely in foil; freeze and use as required. (Makes approximately 16 crêpes.)

4. To make filling, melt 1 tablespoon butter or margarine in medium saucepan over medium heat; add onion and sauté until tender, about 2 minutes. Add turkey, breaking up with fork. Stir in chicken soup, sherry and lemon juice. Reduce heat to low and simmer, covered, for 10 minutes, stirring occasionally.

5. To serve, heat frozen crêpes for 5 minutes in 350° F oven. Place 2 tablespoons filling in each; roll up or fold in half.

TimeSaving Tip: Crêpes are an excellent and elegant commodity to have around for speedy menu preparation. Make and freeze several batches at once; the time you invest in this initial preparation will pay off later in nearly instantaneous main dishes or desserts. Prepare several fillings ahead, too; make some savory and some sweet, and freeze them along with the crêpes. For times when you're really in a hurry, thaw both crêpes and filling for 1 or 2 minutes in the microwave oven; once they're thawed, they're ready to be assembled, reheated and served.

BRIDGE CLUB SUPPER

Asparagus Vinaigrette
Deviled Crab Mornay
Almond Rice
Zucchini
Cherry Crisp

Serves 4.

WORK PLAN: Prepare appetizer: Drain two 16-ounce cans asparagus spears; place asparagus on 4 lettuce-lined salad plates. Top each portion with 2 tablespoons oil and vinegar salad dressing; chill. Cook 1 cup long-grain rice according to label directions; add ¼ cup slivered almonds and keep warm. Prepare Cherry Crisp, then Deviled Crab Mornay (see recipes below). While crab is cooking, heat ¼ cup water, 2 tablespoons butter or margarine and 1 teaspoon salt in large skillet over medium heat; add 4 cups thinly sliced zucchini and simmer, covered, for 5 minutes.

Cherry Crisp

one 21-ounce can cherry pie filling
1 tablespoon lemon juice
½ teaspoon cinnamon
1½ cups granola
1 cup chopped walnuts
¼ cup butter or margarine
1 pint vanilla ice cream

1. In 8 x 8 x 2-inch glass baking dish, blend cherry pie filling, lemon juice and cinnamon. In 4-cup glass measure, mix granola and walnuts; sprinkle over cherry filling.

2. Place butter or margarine in 1-cup glass measure; microwave on high setting for 1 minute to melt. Pour over granola topping.

3. Microwave dessert on high setting for 4 minutes; rotate dish a half turn, then microwave on high setting 4 minutes longer. Serve warm with vanilla ice cream.

Deviled Crab Mornay

2 tablespoons butter or margarine
½ cup chopped onion
2 tablespoons flour
2 tablespoons grated Parmesan cheese
1½ teaspoons dry mustard
¼ teaspoon pepper
1 cup milk
two 6½-ounce packages frozen crabmeat, thawed and drained, or two 6½-ounce cans crabmeat, drained
2 tablespoons dry seasoned bread crumbs
paprika
lemon wedges

1. In 4-cup glass measure, combine butter or margarine and onion. Microwave on high setting for 1 minute.

2. Stir in flour, 1 tablespoon of the grated cheese, the dry mustard and pepper. Blend in milk; mix well. Microwave on high setting for 1½ minutes or until thickened. Stir once during cooking process.

3. Pour ½ cup sauce from measure and reserve. Add drained crabmeat to remaining sauce. Divide mixture among four 10-ounce custard cups or individual soufflé dishes, or place mixture in 1-quart glass casserole.

4. Pour reserved sauce over crabmeat. Sprinkle with mixture of bread crumbs and remaining cheese. Sprinkle lightly with paprika.

5. Microwave on high setting for 5 minutes or on 80% power for 6 minutes, until bubbly. Serve with lemon wedges.

INDIAN SUMMER SPECIAL

Tomato-Onion Salad

Shrimp and Vegetables

White Rice

Honeyed Orange Dessert

Serves 4.

WORK PLAN: Start by preparing salad: Arrange 1 tomato, thinly sliced, and 6 to 8 thin onion rings on each of 4 salad plates. Sprinkle 1 teaspoon each sugar, salt and crumbled basil, 2 tablespoons olive oil and 1 tablespoon lemon juice over each salad and chill. Next, prepare dessert by peeling and slicing 6 oranges; arrange slices in shallow dessert bowl in overlapping circles. Pour mixture of ½ cup honey and ¼ cup orange juice over oranges and sprinkle with ¼ cup each toasted slivered almonds, coarsely chopped walnuts and unsalted cashews or peanuts; chill until ready to serve. Cook 1 cup long-grain rice according to label directions. Prepare Shrimp and Vegetables (see recipe below).

Shrimp and Vegetables

¼ cup vegetable oil

one 16-ounce package frozen shrimp

one 10-ounce package frozen Japanese-style vegetables

1 clove garlic, crushed

2 tablespoons sugar

2 tablespoons soy sauce

2 tablespoons dry vermouth or sherry

1 tablespoon cornstarch

1 tablespoon water

1. Heat oil in large skillet over medium heat; add frozen shrimp, frozen vegetables and garlic and stir-fry for 1 minute. Reduce heat to low and cook, covered, for 2 minutes, stirring once or twice.

2. Add sugar, soy sauce and vermouth or sherry; heat for 30 seconds. Blend cornstarch and water; stir into skillet. Cook until mixture is thickened, about 1 to 2 minutes, stirring constantly.

FANCY EGG SUPPER

Onion Soup

Baked Eggs in Tomato Sauce

Hot Spinach, Bacon and Mushroom Salad

Chocolate Cream Tarts

Serves 4.

WORK PLAN: Make Chocolate Cream Tarts (see recipe below). Prepare salad by mixing 4 cups bite-size pieces fresh spinach leaves with 2 cups thinly sliced mushrooms and 6 fried and crumbled bacon slices. Prepare salad dressing by blending ⅓ cup bacon fat, 3 tablespoons vinegar, 1 teaspoon salt and ½ teaspoon pepper in skillet; heat, and pour over salad just before serving. Heat one 10½-ounce can onion soup according to label directions; keep warm. Serve grated Parmesan cheese to sprinkle over top of soup. Prepare Baked Eggs in Tomato Sauce (see recipe below).

Chocolate Cream Tarts

one 3-ounce package
  chocolate pudding and pie
  filling
2 cups milk
2 teaspoons instant coffee
4 prepared pastry tart shells
½ cup heavy cream
one 1-ounce square chocolate

1. Prepare chocolate pudding and pie mix according to label directions, using 2 cups milk and adding instant coffee. Let stand at room temperature for 15 minutes, beating from time to time to cool as quickly as possible. Spoon into individual pastry shells; chill.

2. Just before serving, beat cream until stiff. Top each tart with whipped cream; sprinkle with chocolate curls made by paring chocolate square, at room temperature, with vegetable parer.

Baked Eggs in Tomato Sauce

one 7¾-ounce individual-
  size can tomato soup
2 teaspoons snipped fresh
  or frozen chives
4 eggs
4 slices American cheese
4 slices whole wheat bread
2 tablespoons butter or
  margarine
2 tablespoons sherry or
  lemon juice

1. Preheat oven to 350° F.

2. Butter four 6-ounce custard cups very well. Place 1 tablespoon undiluted tomato soup in each cup; reserve remaining soup. Sprinkle each portion with ½ teaspoon chives.

3. Break 1 egg into each cup; top each with cheese slice, trimming to fit top of egg. Bake for 15 minutes, until egg white is set and yolk is still soft.

4. Toast bread; butter and cut diagonally into fourths. Heat reserved soup with sherry or lemon juice.

5. Place 4 toast quarters on each serving plate; invert egg on top of toast points, first running sharp knife around egg to loosen from custard cup. Serve soup-sherry mixture alongside as sauce.

**EASY WEEKNIGHT
MENU**

Chicken Soup

Lee's Chinese Pie

Rice

Bean Sprouts with Crisp
Chinese Cabbage

Grapefruit and Orange
Slices

Vanilla Wafers

Serves 4.

WORK PLAN: Prepare dessert by peeling and slicing 2 grapefruit and 2 oranges; arrange slices in shallow dessert dish and chill. Serve with packaged vanilla wafers. Prepare 1 cup long-grain rice according to label directions. Heat one 16-ounce can bean sprouts, rinsed and drained, with 1 cup finely shredded Chinese cabbage over low heat until very hot; keep warm. Prepare Lee's Chinese Pie (see recipe below). Heat one 10¾-ounce can cream of chicken soup according to label directions.

Lee's Chinese Pie

one 10-ounce package
  frozen zucchini slices

4 eggs, beaten

one 4-ounce package
  shredded Cheddar cheese

1 tablespoon instant minced
  onion

½ teaspoon salt

¼ teaspoon pepper

one 3½-ounce can crisp
  Chinese noodles

1. Preheat oven to 350° F.

2. Cook zucchini according to label directions; drain well. Arrange zucchini slices in even layer in lightly greased 9-inch pie plate.

3. Beat together beaten eggs, cheese, minced onion, salt and pepper. Pour mixture over zucchini; sprinkle with Chinese noodles. Bake for 20 minutes or just until set; cut into wedges to serve.

ALL-AMERICAN FAVORITE

Ham and Pea Soup

Macaroni and American Cheese Bake

Red and White Slaw

Peach Pie

Serves 4.

WORK PLAN: First prepare slaw by combining 2 cups finely shredded red cabbage, 2 cups finely shredded white cabbage, ¾ cup sour cream and 2 teaspoons dill seed; chill. Then prepare Macaroni and American Cheese Bake (see recipe below). Place one 18-ounce frozen peach pie in oven with macaroni to thaw and heat. Heat one 10¾-ounce can ham and pea soup according to label directions.

Macaroni and American Cheese Bake

one 8-ounce package elbow
  macaroni

½ cup mayonnaise

½ cup milk

1 tablespoon instant minced
  onion

½ teaspoon salt

¼ teaspoon pepper

one 8-ounce package American
  cheese slices

¼ cup dry unseasoned bread
  crumbs

¼ cup butter or margarine,
  melted

1. Cook macaroni according to label directions; drain.

2. In small bowl, combine mayonnaise, milk, minced onion, salt and pepper.

3. Layer one-third of cooked macaroni in lightly greased 1½-quart casserole, and top with one-third of cheese slices; continue layering macaroni and cheese, one third at a time.

4. Pour mayonnaise-milk mixture over casserole. Sprinkle top with bread crumbs and drizzle with melted butter or margarine. Bake at 350° F for 30 minutes or until casserole is bubbly, cheese is melted and top is crisp.

FONDUE WITH FRIENDS

Hot Chicken Bouillon

Easy Cheese Fondue

French Bread Cubes
Mixed Salad

Fresh Apples and Pears

Serves 4.

2½ cups grated Swiss cheese

1½ tablespoons flour

½ teaspoon dry mustard

¼ teaspoon pepper

2 cups dry white wine

2 to 3 drops hot pepper sauce

WORK PLAN: Place 4 cups bite-size pieces lettuce and ½ cup each tomato wedges, cucumber slices, green pepper strips and thin onion rings in salad bowl; toss with ½ cup red wine vinegar dressing just before serving. Arrange apples and pears for dessert. Heat two 10¾-ounce cans chicken bouillon according to label directions, adding ¼ cup sherry if desired; keep warm. Prepare Easy Cheese Fondue (see recipe below). Serve with French bread cubes.

Easy Cheese Fondue

1. Toss grated cheese with flour, dry mustard and pepper.

2. Bring wine to boiling point in medium-size heavy saucepan over medium heat. Reduce heat to low; add cheese mixture, ½ cup at a time, stirring to melt cheese after each addition. Add hot pepper sauce; stir well. Serve immediately, placing on trivet over canned heat source.

MARVELOUS MEATLESS MEAL

Spinach Soup

Triple Cheese Noodle Pie

Zucchini and Cauliflower

Walnut Ice Cream
Butter Cookies

Serves 4.

one 8-ounce package spiral-shaped noodles

one 16-ounce container ricotta or small curd cottage cheese

2 cups shredded mozzarella cheese

2 tablespoons chopped parsley

½ teaspoon salt

½ teaspoon oregano

¼ teaspoon pepper

one 15½-ounce jar spaghetti sauce

2 tablespoons grated Parmesan cheese

WORK PLAN: Prepare dessert by making 4 large scoops out of 1½ pints vanilla ice cream. Press broken walnut pieces over all; set one in each of 4 dessert dishes and freeze. Serve with butter cookies. Make Triple Cheese Noodle Pie (see recipe below). Prepare one 10-ounce package frozen zucchini and one 10-ounce package frozen cauliflower according to label directions; drain, and toss with ¼ cup chopped parsley. Heat one 10¾-ounce can chicken bouillon according to label directions, adding 1 cup finely shredded spinach.

Triple Cheese Noodle Pie

1. Cook noodles according to label directions; drain.

2. In large bowl, mix ricotta or cottage cheese, mozzarella cheese, parsley, salt, oregano and pepper. Gently fold in cooked noodles and 1½ cups of the spaghetti sauce.

3. Spoon mixture into lightly greased 2-quart casserole; top with remaining sauce and sprinkle with Parmesan cheese. Bake at 350° F for 20 to 25 minutes or until bubbly and lightly browned.

Quick Winter Meals

Nothing is as gratifying on an icy cold day as a steaming bowl of hot soup, a thick, savory stew or a warm, stick-to-the-ribs dessert like hot gingerbread or warm cherry pudding.

Here they all are, the quick winter warm-ups made for the days you're cold and hungry—and in a hurry. This chapter includes hearty main courses like Shepherd's Beef Pie and Mustard Veal Rolls, all mixed and matched with soups, salads and seasonal desserts.

When the holidays are upon you and you're busy with shopping and parties, don't worry about dinner. The planning has all been done for you here. For New Year's at home, for example, the festive "Dinner for New Year's Eve" is elegant and easy: Pâté with Crackers, Grilled Parslied Lamb Chops, Duchess Potatoes, Zucchini and Pea Casserole, and Grapes with Brie Cheese.

Or perhaps the cold puts you in the mood for a "Chalet Supper": G'Roestl (sautéed beef and potatoes flavored with caraway seeds) accompanied by Buttered Fennel and Creamed Spinach. For dessert there's Kaiserschmarren, a giant rolled pancake filled with raspberry jam and topped with whipped cream.

Whether you're skiing, skating, sledding or just warming yourself by the fire while the winter winds howl outside, it's great to know you can have a delicious, hot meal on the table in minutes.

COMPANY FONDUE

Beef Fondue

Hot Crusty Bread
Green Salad

Pears in Marsala
Macaroons

Serves 4.

WORK PLAN: To prepare dessert, divide one 20-ounce can pear halves among 4 individual dessert dishes. Pour 2 to 3 tablespoons Marsala or sweet sherry wine over each serving; chill, and serve with store-bought macaroons. In large salad bowl, toss together 6 cups mixed salad greens (lettuce, watercress, spinach, endive); add ½ cup oil and vinegar salad dressing just before serving. Wrap crusty French or Italian bread in foil; heat in oven while preparing Beef Fondue (see recipe below).

Beef Fondue

2 **pounds sirloin steak**
vegetable oil
½ **cup butter**

    HORSERADISH SAUCE

½ **cup sour cream**
2 **teaspoons horseradish**

    CREAMY ITALIAN SAUCE

½ **cup creamy Italian-style dressing**
1 **tablespoon snipped fresh or frozen chives**

    MUSTARD SAUCE

½ **cup mayonnaise**
3 **tablespoons prepared spicy mustard**

    CAPER SAUCE

½ **cup bottled steak sauce**
2 **tablespoons capers, drained**

1. Trim steak and cut into 1-inch cubes. Arrange sirloin cubes on large platter. Pour oil into fondue pot or electric skillet to depth of 1½ inches. Set butter on small plate beside pan.

2. Blend ingredients for each sauce. Divide sauces among 4 fondue plates with separate sections for sauces, or place sauces in 16 tiny dishes and give each diner 4 sauces on a large dinner plate.

3. Heat oil to 375° F; add butter. Carefully place pot on trivet over canned heat source. Spear meat cubes with fondue forks; fry until done. Dip into sauces.

FESTIVE COLD-WEATHER DINING

Broiled Shell Steaks

Long-Grain and Wild Rice
Browned-Butter Sprouts

Gingerbread with
Applesauce

Serves 4.

WORK PLAN: For dessert, prepare one 14-ounce package gingerbread mix according to label directions; serve topped with hot applesauce. Prepare one 6¾-ounce package long-grain and wild rice mix according to label directions. Prepare two 10-ounce packages frozen Brussels sprouts according to label directions; keep warm, and toss with 2 tablespoons each browned butter and lemon juice just before serving. Prepare Broiled Shell Steaks (see recipe below).

Broiled Shell Steaks

4 shell steaks, about
¾ inch thick

½ cup Italian-style salad
dressing

1 tablespoon lemon juice

1. Preheat broiler.

2. Wipe steaks with damp paper towels; place steaks in shallow baking dish. Pour in salad dressing and lemon juice. Marinate steaks at room temperature for 10 minutes, turning occasionally.

3. Broil steaks 4 inches from heat, 4 to 7 minutes per side.

CANDLELIGHT DELIGHT

Skillet Stroganoff

Egg Noodles
Braised Celery and Carrots

Cherries Jubilee

Serves 4.

WORK PLAN: To prepare dessert, divide 1½ pints vanilla ice cream among 4 individual dessert dishes; freeze. Blend 2 tablespoons cornstarch with juice from one 16-ounce can sweetened Bing cherries in small saucepan; heat to boiling point, stirring constantly. Add cherries and keep warm. At dessert time, heat ½ cup rum in small skillet; ignite and stir, while flaming, into cherry sauce. Spoon over ice cream and serve immediately. Prepare vegetable by cooking 2 cups each julienne strips celery and carrots in ½ cup chicken broth and 2 tablespoons butter or margarine until tender, about 10 minutes; keep warm. Prepare Skillet Stroganoff (see recipe below). Meanwhile, cook one 16-ounce package egg noodles according to label directions.

Skillet Stroganoff

1½ pounds sirloin steak

2 tablespoons vegetable oil

2 tablespoons butter or
margarine

1 cup chopped onion

one 6-ounce can sliced
mushrooms, drained

2 cups sour cream

1 tablespoon tomato paste

1 tablespoon sherry

1 teaspoon salt

¼ teaspoon pepper

¼ cup chopped parsley

1. Wipe steak with damp paper towels; cut steak into thin strips. Heat oil and butter or margarine in large skillet over medium heat; add steak strips and sauté on both sides until brown, about 2 minutes. Remove from skillet with slotted spoon; set aside.

2. Add onion to drippings in skillet; sauté until tender, about 2 minutes, stirring constantly. Reduce heat to low; stir in drained mushrooms, sour cream, tomato paste, sherry, salt and pepper.

3. Return meat to skillet; heat until very hot, about 5 minutes, stirring constantly (do not boil). Sprinkle with parsley.

DOUBLE-QUICK DINNER DELUXE

Deluxe Hamburger au Poivre

Parslied Rice
Garden Salad

Garlic Bread

Peaches and Pouring Cream

Serves 4.

WORK PLAN: Divide one 20-ounce can cling peach halves among 4 dessert dishes and pour 1 cup heavy cream into pitcher; chill until dessert time. Tear 4 cups mixed salad greens into bite-size pieces; add 2 tomatoes, cut into wedges, and ½ cup thin cucumber slices; toss and chill. Add oil and vinegar dressing just before serving. Slice French bread into ½-inch slices and spread both sides of each with garlic spread; reassemble into loaf, wrap in foil and heat in 300° F oven. Make Deluxe Hamburger au Poivre (see recipe below). Prepare quick-cooking rice according to label directions to yield 4 servings, adding ¼ cup chopped parsley. *Shown on page 71.*

Deluxe Hamburger au Poivre

2 **pounds lean ground beef (sirloin or round)**

1 **egg, beaten**

1 **teaspoon Worcestershire sauce**

½ **teaspoon curry powder**

2 **tablespoons lemon pepper**

2 **tablespoons butter or margarine**

chopped parsley

1. In large bowl, combine ground beef, beaten egg, Worcestershire sauce and curry; mix well.

2. Divide meat into 4 portions; form into oblong "steaks" about 1 inch thick. Sprinkle both sides of each portion with lemon pepper; press lightly into meat.

3. Melt butter or margarine in large heavy skillet over medium heat; add meat and sauté until well browned, 3 to 7 minutes per side.

4. Place steaks on individual serving plates and pour some pan juices over each. Sprinkle with parsley.

SCOUT NIGHT SUPPER

New England Clam Chowder

Hamburger Biscuit Bake

Apple-Pineapple Salad Supreme

Chocolate Pudding Dessert
Vanilla Cookies

Serves 4.

WORK PLAN: Prepare Hamburger Biscuit Bake (see recipe below). While it's baking, prepare salad by combining 2 cups apple slices, one 8-ounce can pineapple chunks, drained, ½ cup chopped walnuts, ¼ cup mayonnaise, ¼ cup sour cream and 1½ teaspoons salt; place in lettuce-lined salad bowl and chill. Place chocolate pudding from one 5-ounce individual-size can in each of 4 dessert dishes; chill, and serve with vanilla cookies. Heat one 10¾-ounce can New England-style clam chowder according to label directions.

Hamburger Biscuit Bake

1½ pounds ground beef
½ cup finely chopped celery
one 17-ounce can corn
  niblets, drained
one 3-ounce can French-
  fried onion rings
½ teaspoon salt
¼ teaspoon garlic powder
½ cup beef broth
2 cups packaged biscuit mix
½ cup cold water
paprika

1. Preheat oven to 425° F.

2. Brown ground beef and celery in large skillet over medium heat for 4 to 5 minutes, stirring constantly. Drain surplus fat from skillet.

3. Add drained corn niblets, onion rings, salt and garlic powder to beef mixture in skillet; mix well. Stir in beef broth. Pour mixture into lightly greased 1½-quart casserole.

4. Prepare biscuit mix according to label directions, using ½ cup cold water. Spoon mixture evenly over meat mixture to make crust; sprinkle with paprika. Bake for 25 to 30 minutes or until meat mixture bubbles and biscuit crust is golden brown.

**DINING
DANISH STYLE**

Herring and Onions in Sour
Cream

Open-Face Danish Burgers

Julienne Beets
Sugar Peas

Prune and Apricot Compote

Spice Cookies

Serves 4.

WORK PLAN: Prepare Prune and Apricot Compote (see recipe below), and serve for dessert with store-bought spice cookies. Prepare appetizer by draining two 6-ounce jars herring in wine sauce and combining herring with 2 cups thin onion rings and 1 cup sour cream. Divide among 4 salad plates and chill. Cook two 10-ounce packages frozen peas according to label directions, adding 2 teaspoons sugar to cooking liquid. Heat two 16-ounce cans julienne beets according to label directions; keep vegetables warm while making Open-Face Danish Burgers (see recipe below).

Prune and Apricot Compote

1 cup dried pitted prunes
1 cup dried apricot halves
½ cup brown sugar
1 lemon, sliced
two 2-inch cinnamon sticks

1. In medium saucepan, combine prunes, apricot halves and brown sugar. Add water to cover. Bring to boiling point over medium heat; reduce heat to low and add lemon and cinnamon sticks.

2. Simmer, covered, for 20 minutes or until fruit is tender. Serve compote warm.

Open-Face Danish Burgers

1½ pounds ground round

1 teaspoon Worcestershire sauce

½ teaspoon pepper

2 hard-cooked eggs, sliced

¼ cup mayonnaise

¼ cup butter or margarine

4 slices rye bread

one 2-ounce can flat anchovy fillets

¼ cup chopped parsley

8 lemon wedges

1. In medium bowl, blend ground beef, Worcestershire sauce and pepper. Form into eight 3 x 4-inch ovals. Top 4 patties with egg slices, arranging in overlapping line down center of each. Top each with 1 tablespoon mayonnaise, spreading gently to cover. Top with remaining patties; press edges to seal.

2. Melt 2 tablespoons of the butter or margarine in large skillet over medium heat; add hamburgers and sauté, 2 to 6 minutes per side.

3. Toast rye bread; spread with remaining butter or margarine. Top each slice with cooked hamburger and top each burger with 2 anchovy fillets. Sprinkle each with 1 tablespoon parsley; garnish each burger with 2 lemon wedges.

AFTER-THEATER DINNER

Burgundy Beef Balls

Herbed Rice
String Beans

Pear-Walnut Torte

Serves 4.

WORK PLAN: Start by preparing dessert: Drain one 32-ounce can pear halves; cut pears into thin slices and toss with 1 cup chopped walnuts. Layer into a 9-inch ready-to-serve pastry shell; pour 1 cup apricot preserves, melted, over pears. Chill, and serve with 1 cup heavy cream, stiffly beaten. Cook 1 cup long-grain rice according to label directions; stir in 2 tablespoons each chopped parsley, snipped dill and chives, or 1½ teaspoons each dried herbs. Prepare one 16-ounce polybag frozen string beans according to label directions. Prepare Burgundy Beef Balls (see recipe below).

Burgundy Beef Balls

1 pound boneless lean beef, cut into 1-inch cubes

1 medium onion, peeled and quartered

1 slice white bread, quartered

6 parsley sprigs

1 teaspoon salt

1 egg

2 tablespoons butter or margarine

one 10¾-ounce can golden mushroom soup

½ cup red Burgundy wine

½ cup water

1. With steel all-purpose blade in place in food processor, place half of beef in food processor bowl. Chop finely by rapidly turning machine on and off for 5 seconds. Place chopped meat in mixing bowl; process remaining beef the same way and add to mixing bowl.

2. Place onion, bread, parsley, salt and egg in food processor bowl. Process until well mixed by turning machine on and off for 10 seconds. Add ground beef to food processor; process until well mixed by turning machine on and off for 10 seconds. Shape mixture into 1-inch meatballs.

3. Melt butter or margarine in large skillet over medium heat; add meatballs and sauté for about 7 to 10 minutes, turning to brown all sides and cook through. Remove to heated serving platter; keep warm. Drain surplus fat from skillet.

4. Blend soup, wine and water in same skillet. Bring to boiling point; reduce heat to low and simmer for 2 minutes, stirring constantly to blend into pan drippings. Pour over beef balls.

CHALET SUPPER

G'Roestl

Buttered Fennel
Creamy Spinach

Kaiserschmarren

Serves 4.

WORK PLAN: Cook 4 cups julienne strips fennel in boiling salted water; drain, and toss with 2 tablespoons butter or margarine. Prepare two 10-ounce packages frozen chopped spinach according to label directions; drain, then stir in ¼ cup heavy cream, 2 tablespoons butter or margarine and ¼ teaspoon nutmeg. Keep vegetables warm. Prepare G'Roestl (see recipe below). For dessert, mix ¾ cup packaged pancake mix according to label directions; fry batter in large skillet as 1 large pancake. When second side is cooked and pancake is still in skillet, spread generously with raspberry jam. Roll up jelly-roll fashion, sprinkle with cinnamon sugar and serve at once, topped with ½ cup heavy cream, stiffly beaten.

G'Roestl

2 cups diced peeled potatoes

2 tablespoons butter or margarine

½ cup chopped onion

2 cups cubed cooked roast beef

1 teaspoon caraway seeds

½ teaspoon salt

¼ teaspoon pepper

1. Add potatoes to boiling salted water in medium saucepan over medium heat; cook until tender, about 10 minutes. Drain.

2. Melt butter or margarine in large skillet over medium heat; add onion and sauté until tender, about 4 minutes, stirring constantly.

3. Add potatoes to onion in skillet; sauté until potatoes are golden brown, about 5 minutes, stirring occasionally. Add beef, caraway seeds, salt and pepper; cook for about 2 to 3 minutes, until heated through, stirring occasionally.

FAR EAST FEAST

Spiced Beef Bouillon

Meatballs with Chinese Vegetables

Egg Noodles with Green Onions

Chilled Golden Figs

Cinnamon Cookies

Serves 4.

WORK PLAN: Begin by dividing two 10½-ounce cans beef bouillon among 4 glasses; add 2 to 3 drops hot pepper sauce to each and chill. Divide one 16-ounce can golden figs and one 8-ounce can green grapes among 4 dessert dishes; chill, and serve for dessert with store-bought cinnamon cookies. Make Meatballs with Chinese Vegetables (see recipe below). At the same time, prepare one 16-ounce package egg noodles according to label directions. Melt 2 tablespoons butter or margarine in small skillet over medium heat; add 1 cup sliced green onions and sauté for 2 minutes. Add onions with pan drippings to drained noodles; toss to combine.

Meatballs with Chinese Vegetables

½ cup water

¼ cup uncooked long-grain rice

1 pound ground round beef

¼ cup finely chopped water chestnuts

one ¾-ounce package onion soup mix

1 egg, beaten

2 tablespoons vegetable oil

one 10-ounce package frozen Chinese-style vegetables

one 8-ounce can bamboo shoots, drained

2 tablespoons soy sauce

1. Bring water to boiling point in small saucepan over medium heat; stir in rice. Reduce heat to low and simmer, covered, for 15 minutes or until rice is tender. Cool slightly.

2. In medium bowl, combine ground beef, water chestnuts, onion soup mix, beaten egg and cooked rice. Blend well; shape mixture into 1-inch meatballs.

3. Heat oil in large skillet over medium heat; add meatballs and sauté for about 5 minutes, turning to brown all sides.

4. Stir in frozen vegetables; reduce heat to low and cook, covered, for 3 minutes, stirring occasionally. Add drained bamboo shoots and soy sauce. Cook 30 seconds longer, stirring constantly.

SUPERBOWL SUNDAY SUPPER

Western Rice and Beef

Fresh Mushroom Salad

Dessert Blini

Serves 4.

½ cup uncooked long-grain rice

2 tablespoons butter or margarine

½ cup chopped onion

¼ cup chopped green pepper

1 pound ground beef

one 16-ounce can stewed tomatoes

¼ cup chili sauce

¼ cup chopped black olives

1 cup grated Monterey Jack or mozzarella cheese

WORK PLAN: Chill 4 cups sliced fresh mushrooms. Just before serving, toss with ⅓ cup each garlic dressing and chopped parsley. Prepare Western Rice and Beef (see recipe below). Make Blini at dessert time (see recipe below).

Western Rice and Beef

1. Cook rice according to label directions. Meanwhile, melt butter or margarine in large skillet over medium heat; add onion and green pepper and sauté until onion is golden, about 4 minutes.

2. Add ground beef; cook until meat loses its pink color, stirring to break meat into small pieces. Stir in tomatoes, chili sauce, black olives and cooked rice.

3. Reduce heat to low and simmer, covered, for 10 minutes. Sprinkle with grated cheese; heat, covered, 2 minutes longer, just until cheese is melted.

Dessert Blini

8 crêpes, 6 inches in diameter, prepared ahead and frozen

1 cup small curd cottage cheese

1 egg, slightly beaten

¼ cup golden raisins

2 tablespoons sugar

1 teaspoon cinnamon

2 tablespoons butter or margarine

½ cup sour cream

1. Remove prepared crêpes from freezer to thaw.

2. In small bowl, mix together cottage cheese, slightly beaten egg, golden raisins, sugar and cinnamon. Spoon 2 tablespoons mixture into center of each crêpe. Fold two parallel sides of crêpe toward center to contain filling; roll up jelly-roll fashion.

3. Melt butter or margarine in large skillet over medium heat; add blini and fry until lightly browned on all sides.

4. Place 2 blini on each of 4 dessert plates; top each with a little sour cream and serve immediately.

POSH POTLUCK MEAL

Cream of Celery Soup

Shepherd's Beef Pie

Sliced Tomato Salad

Quick Tapioca Parfaits

Serves 4.

WORK PLAN: Prepare Shepherd's Beef Pie (see recipe below). Make dessert by preparing one 3¼-ounce package instant tapioca according to label directions; allow to cool slightly, then fold in 1 stiffly beaten egg white and 1 teaspoon grated lemon rind. Place drained apricot halves from one 8-ounce can in bottom of 4 parfait glasses; top with tapioca and chill. Place a thinly sliced tomato on each of 4 salad plates; spoon 1 tablespoon garlic dressing over each. Heat one 10¾-ounce can cream of celery soup according to label directions.

Shepherd's Beef Pie

1 pound lean ground beef

one 17-ounce can cut green beans, drained

¼ cup chopped parsley

1 tablespoon instant minced onion

½ teaspoon salt

¼ teaspoon pepper

1⅓ cups instant mashed potatoes

2 tablespoons grated Parmesan cheese

1. In large bowl, gently mix ground beef, drained green beans, parsley, minced onion, salt and pepper. Press mixture into lightly greased 9-inch pie plate.

2. Prepare instant mashed potatoes to yield 4 servings. Spread warm potatoes over beef mixture; sprinkle with grated cheese. Bake at 400° F for 25 to 30 minutes or until meat is thoroughly cooked and potatoes are golden.

NOTE: Use either ground round or sirloin in this recipe.

DANDY HAMBURGER DINNER

Relish Tray

Hamburger Stroganoff

Buttered Green Noodles
Parslied Carrots

Vanilla Ice Cream with
Raspberry Melba Sauce

Serves 4.

WORK PLAN: Divide 1½ pints vanilla ice cream among 4 dessert dishes; set in freezer. Prepare sauce by placing frozen raspberries from one 12-ounce package along with 2 tablespoons red currant jelly in electric blender; puree, then chill. Pour sauce over ice cream when ready to serve. Prepare relish tray of black and green olives, washed whole radishes and celery sticks; chill. Prepare Hamburger Stroganoff (see recipe below). Cook one 16-ounce polybag frozen baby carrots according to label directions; drain, then toss with 2 tablespoons butter or margarine and 2 tablespoons chopped parsley. Cook one 16-ounce package green noodles according to label directions; drain, then toss with 2 tablespoons butter or margarine.

Hamburger Stroganoff

2 tablespoons butter or margarine

½ cup finely chopped onion

1½ pounds ground beef

⅛ teaspoon garlic powder

one 6-ounce can mushrooms, drained

½ cup beef broth

¼ cup sherry

1 tablespoon lemon juice

1 cup sour cream

1. Melt butter or margarine in large skillet over medium heat; add onion and sauté until tender and golden, about 3 to 4 minutes. Add ground beef and garlic powder; cook for 4 to 5 minutes, stirring constantly to break meat into small pieces. Drain surplus fat from skillet.

2. Reduce heat to low; add drained mushrooms, beef broth, sherry and lemon juice to beef mixture in skillet. Simmer, covered, for 10 minutes.

3. Blend in sour cream; cook 1 to 2 minutes longer, stirring constantly (do not boil).

SUPER SKIERS' SUPPER

Mustard Veal Rolls

Dilled Potatoes
Hot Cucumbers

Mincemeat Ice Cream

Serves 4.

WORK PLAN: Prepare dessert by dividing 1½ pints vanilla ice cream among 4 individual dessert glasses. Top each serving with 2 tablespoons prepared mincemeat; freeze. Prepare Mustard Veal Rolls (see recipe below). Meanwhile, peel 1 pound potatoes and cut them into quarters; cook in boiling salted water until tender. Toss potatoes with 2 tablespoons butter or margarine and 1 tablespoon dried dill; keep warm. Pare and seed 3 cucumbers and cut into julienne strips; cook in ¼ cup chicken broth and ¼ teaspoon each salt and nutmeg until just tender, about 3 to 5 minutes.

Mustard Veal Rolls

1 pound veal, thinly sliced
  (4 pieces)
¼ cup Dijon-style mustard
4 slices precooked ham
4 slices Swiss cheese
¼ cup flour
2 tablespoons butter or
  margarine
½ cup dry white wine
1 tablespoon tomato paste
½ teaspoon basil

1. Wipe veal with damp paper towels. Place each piece between two sheets of waxed paper; using wooden mallet or rolling pin, pound very thin (or have your butcher do this).

2. Spread one side of each piece of veal with a little mustard. Place ham slice on top of each. Spread with a little more mustard. Place cheese slice on top of each ham slice and spread with remaining mustard.

3. Roll up each piece jelly-roll fashion, securing seams with toothpicks. Sprinkle each roll with a little flour.

4. Melt butter or margarine in large skillet over medium heat; add veal rolls and sauté for about 4 minutes, turning to brown all sides. Reduce heat to low.

5. Beat together wine, tomato paste and basil; pour around rolls. Simmer, covered, for 15 to 20 minutes or until tender.

**MINUTES-ONLY
MENU**

Hot and Sour Mushroom
Soup

Shredded Pork and Cabbage

Herb and Wild Rice

Coconut Custard

Serves 4.

WORK PLAN: First make dessert: Prepare one 3¾-ounce package instant vanilla pudding and pie filling according to label directions; stir in one 3-ounce can flaked coconut. Divide among 4 dessert dishes; chill. Next, prepare soup by heating one 10¾-ounce can golden mushroom soup with ½ cup beef broth, ¼ cup soy sauce and ¼ cup red wine vinegar; keep warm. Prepare one 6-ounce package herb and wild rice mix according label directions, and make Shredded Pork and Cabbage (see recipe below).

Shredded Pork and Cabbage

1 pound lean pork shoulder
¼ cup vegetable oil
4 cups finely shredded
  cabbage
¼ cup soy sauce
1 tablespoon brown sugar
one 3-ounce can French-
  fried onion rings

1. Wipe pork well with damp paper towels; cut meat into julienne strips. Heat oil in large skillet, electric skillet or wok; add pork and stir-fry until browned, about 2 minutes.

2. Add cabbage; stir-fry until slightly wilted, about 3 minutes. Add soy sauce and brown sugar; stir-fry 1 minute longer. Add onion rings; stir and heat for 30 seconds.

COZY FRENCH SUPPER

Cassoulet Alsace

Garlic Bread
Butter Lettuce Salad

Apple Tarte

Serves 4.

WORK PLAN: Prepare Apple Tarte and Cassoulet Alsace (see recipes below). Cut a long loaf of crusty French bread into ½-inch-thick slices to within ¼ inch of bottom of loaf; spread each cut side with a little of ¼ cup softened butter or margarine blended with 1 clove garlic, crushed. Wrap in foil; heat for 5 minutes alongside cassoulet. To prepare salad, wash and dry 2 small heads Boston lettuce; arrange whole tiny leaves on 4 individual salad plates and sprinkle each with some of ½ cup chopped walnuts. Make dressing of ½ cup olive oil, ¼ cup lemon juice and 1 teaspoon each salt, sugar and Dijon-style mustard; spoon some over each salad.

Cassoulet Alsace

4 pork loin chops, boned

2-pound kielbasa or garlic sausage ring

1 tablespoon vegetable oil

two 20-ounce cans cannellini or navy beans

one 8-ounce can tomato sauce

½ cup red wine

½ cup grated carrot

¼ cup chopped parsley

one ¾-ounce package onion soup mix

½ teaspoon thyme

1. Wipe pork chops and sausage with damp paper towels; cut chops into 1-inch pieces and sausage into 2-inch pieces. Heat oil in large skillet over medium heat; add pork and sausage pieces and sauté for about 4 to 5 minutes, stirring occasionally.

2. Meanwhile, combine undrained beans, tomato sauce, wine, carrot, parsley, onion soup mix and thyme in 2-quart casserole. Add browned meats and pan drippings; stir to mix well. Bake at 450° F for 30 minutes.

Apple Tarte

one 9-inch frozen prepared pie shell

3 tablespoons sugar

1 cup sweetened applesauce

2 cups sliced peeled apples

2 tablespoons red currant jelly

1. Preheat oven to 450° F.

2. Sprinkle bottom of pie shell with 1 tablespoon of the sugar. Spread applesauce over bottom of shell. Arrange apple slices on top of applesauce in overlapping spiral, working from center to edge.

3. Sprinkle with remaining sugar and dot with jelly. Place tarte in oven with cassoulet; bake for 25 minutes.

DINNER IN NO TIME

Tomato Consommé

Pork Fried Rice

Sautéed Mushrooms

Vanilla Ice Cream with Plum Sauce

Serves 4.

WORK PLAN: To make dessert; divide 1½ pints vanilla ice cream among 4 large parfait glasses; freeze. Make sauce by draining juice from one 20-ounce can purple plums and discarding stones from plums; puree plums in electric blender at high speed. Chill plum puree and spoon over ice cream just before serving. Heat two 10-ounce cans consommé Madrilène; keep warm. Prepare Pork Fried Rice (see recipe below). Heat 2 tablespoons oil in large skillet over medium heat; add 6 cups thinly sliced mushrooms and 2 tablespoons each soy sauce and lemon juice. Cook until mushrooms are tender.

Pork Fried Rice

1 cup uncooked long-grain rice

3 tablespoons vegetable oil

½ cup julienne strips cooked pork

one ¾-ounce package onion soup mix

2 eggs, beaten

1. Cook rice according to label directions in medium skillet. Cool slightly.

2. Heat oil in large skillet, electric skillet or wok at medium heat. Add cooked rice, pork and onion soup mix. Stir to blend well. Cook for 2 minutes, stirring constantly.

3. Form hollow in center of rice mixture and pour in beaten eggs. Stir eggs until they are thickened and slightly set, then stir eggs into rice mixture.

NOTE: This is an ideal use for leftover pork.

SNOW SHOVELERS' REWARD

Ham with Black Cherry Sauce

Buttered Potatoes
Mixed Vegetables

Seven-Layer Cake

Serves 4.

WORK PLAN: To prepare dessert, cut one 12-ounce store-bought pound cake horizontally into 7 layers; spread 2 tablespoons raspberry preserves between each layer. Frost with 1 cup heavy cream, stiffly beaten and sweetened with 2 tablespoons confectioners' sugar; chill until serving time. Peel 1½ pounds potatoes and cut into ½-inch-thick slices; cook in boiling salted water until tender, about 15 minutes. Drain, then toss with 2 tablespoons butter or margarine; keep warm. Cook one 16-ounce polybag frozen mixed vegetables according to label directions; keep warm. Prepare Ham with Black Cherry Sauce (see recipe below).

Ham with Black Cherry Sauce

two ¾-pound precooked
  ham steaks, ½ inch thick
one 12-ounce can pitted
  black cherries
1 tablespoon cornstarch
1 tablespoon brown sugar
1 tablespoon lemon juice
¼ teaspoon ginger
¼ teaspoon cinnamon

1. Wipe ham steaks well with damp paper towels. Place steaks side by side in 13 x 9 x 2-inch glass baking dish; set aside.

2. Drain cherries, reserving ¼ cup juice. In 4-cup glass measure, blend cornstarch and reserved juice. Stir in brown sugar, lemon juice, ginger and cinnamon.

3. Microwave on high setting for 2 minutes to thicken. Stir once during cooking process. Pour over ham; cover dish with waxed paper.

4. Microwave on high setting for 5 minutes; spoon cherry sauce and pan juices over ham. Re-cover dish and microwave on high setting 5 minutes longer. Let stand, covered, at room temperature for 3 minutes before serving.

**EVERYONE'S-BUSY-TONIGHT
SUPPER**
Ham Patties with Pineapple
Lemony Broccoli
Almond Pie Delight
Serves 4.

WORK PLAN: Prepare Almond Pie Delight (see recipe below). Cook two 10-ounce packages frozen chopped broccoli according to label directions; drain, and toss with 2 tablespoons butter or margarine, 2 tablespoons lemon juice and 1 teaspoon grated lemon rind. Keep warm while making Ham Patties with Pineapple (see recipe below).

Almond Delight Pie

1 cup sugar
1 cup slivered almonds
½ cup golden raisins
½ cup soda cracker crumbs
3 egg whites
1 teaspoon almond extract
1 cup heavy cream
2 tablespoons confectioners'
  sugar
1 tablespoon sherry
  (optional)

1. Preheat oven to 350° F.

2. In large bowl, combine sugar, ½ cup of the slivered almonds, the golden raisins and cracker crumbs.

3. In another large bowl, beat egg whites until stiff. Fold into almond-cracker mixture along with almond extract. Spoon into well-greased 9-inch pie plate. Bake for 30 minutes or until brown.

4. Meanwhile, beat cream until stiff; fold in remaining ½ cup almonds, the confectioners' sugar, and sherry if desired. Chill until serving time. Serve alongside warm dessert.

Ham Patties with Pineapple

one 8-ounce can pineapple
  rings

2 tablespoons ketchup

1 teaspoon brown sugar

one 16-ounce can ham
  patties (8 patties)

2 English muffins, split and
  toasted

1. Preheat broiler.

2. Drain pineapple rings; reserve 2 tablespoons juice. Set rings aside.

3. In small bowl, blend ketchup, brown sugar and reserved juice. Broil ham patties 4 inches from heat until lightly browned. Turn patties to other side.

4. Top 4 of the patties with pineapple rings; brush pineapple rings and surfaces of other patties with glaze. Broil 3 to 4 minutes longer. Place 4 plain patties glazed side up on top of pineapple rings. Set each on toasted English muffin half.

**JIFFY
GERMAN DINNER**

**Mock Sauerbraten in Red
Wine Gravy**

Quick Potato Dumplings

Savory Beets

Hot Plums
Ginger Cookies

Serves 4.

WORK PLAN: Heat sliced beets from one 16-ounce jar, stirring in 1 teaspoon each grated orange rind and lemon rind; keep warm. Heat whole purple plums from one 20-ounce can; keep warm, and serve for dessert with store-bought ginger cookies. Prepare Mock Sauerbraten in Red Wine Gravy and serve with Quick Potato Dumplings (see recipes below).

Mock Sauerbraten in Red Wine Gravy

4 large or 8 small bratwurst

2 tablespoons butter or
  margarine

½ cup finely chopped
  onion

one ⅞-ounce package
  brown gravy mix

1 cup dry red wine

½ cup water

1 teaspoon sugar

1. Prick bratwurst very well with fork; place in 2 inches cold water in large saucepan. Bring to boiling point over medium heat; reduce heat to low and simmer, covered, for 5 minutes. Drain.

2. Melt butter or margarine in large skillet over medium heat; add onion and bratwurst and sauté until brown, about 5 minutes. Remove bratwurst and set aside.

3. Blend brown gravy mix with onion and drippings in skillet; add wine, ½ cup water and the sugar. Bring to boiling point, stirring constantly.

4. Return bratwurst to skillet; reduce heat to low and simmer, covered, for 5 minutes.

Quick Potato Dumplings

½ cup water

¼ cup milk

3 tablespoons instant mashed potatoes

1 egg

1 tablespoon chopped parsley

½ teaspoon salt

¼ teaspoon pepper

¼ cup dry unseasoned bread crumbs

¼ cup flour

1. Heat water and milk and add instant mashed potatoes; cook according to label directions.

2. Beat in egg, parsley, salt and pepper. Stir in bread crumbs and flour to make stiff batter.

3. Bring 2 inches salted water to boiling point in large saucepan; drop batter by tablespoonfuls into water. Boil for 10 minutes; remove from water with slotted spoon.

BLACK FOREST MENU

Hot German Potato Salad

Sautéed Bratwurst

Carrots and Parsnips

Wine Cream

Serves 4.

WORK PLAN: To prepare dessert, cook one 3¾-ounce package vanilla pudding and pie filling according to label directions using 1½ cups milk; cool. Stir in ½ cup white wine; fold in 2 stiffly beaten egg whites. Divide Wine Cream among 4 dessert glasses and chill. Prepare Hot German Potato Salad and Sautéed Bratwurst (see recipes below). Cook 2 cups each julienne strips carrots and parsnips in boiling salted water for 10 minutes, until tender; drain.

Hot German Potato Salad

2½ cups water

one 5½-ounce package scalloped potato mix

2 slices bacon, cut into 1-inch pieces

¼ cup chopped onion

1 envelope beef powder concentrate

¼ cup vinegar

¼ cup chopped parsley

1 tablespoon mild paprika

1. Bring water to boiling point in medium saucepan over medium heat; add dehydrated potato slices. (Reserve package of sauce mix for another use.) Reduce heat to low and simmer, covered, for 10 to 15 minutes or until potatoes are tender.

2. Fry bacon pieces in large skillet over medium heat until slightly curled. Add onion; sauté until onion is tender, about 5 minutes, stirring constantly.

3. Add beef concentrate and vinegar to bacon-onion mixture. Bring to boiling point; stir in potato slices. Remove from heat; stir gently to mix well. Mound in center of large heated serving platter. Sprinkle with parsley and paprika. Surround with Sautéed Bratwurst.

Sautéed Bratwurst

2 pounds bratwurst
¼ cup butter or margarine
2 cups sliced onions
1½ teaspoons caraway
seeds

1. Prick bratwurst well with fork. Place in large saucepan; add water to cover. Bring to boiling point over medium heat. Remove from heat; cover and let stand.

2. Melt butter or margarine in large skillet over medium heat; add onions and sauté until tender and golden, about 5 minutes, stirring constantly. Stir in caraway seeds.

3. Remove bratwurst from water and add to onions; sauté bratwurst and onions until bratwurst is golden brown on all sides. Place around Hot German Potato Salad.

**HOLIDAY SHOPPERS'
SUPPER**

Chicken Vegetable Soup

**Sausages and Peppers in
Pita Pockets**

Warm Cherry Pudding

Serves 4.

WORK PLAN: Prepare Warm Cherry Pudding and Sausages and Peppers in Pita Pockets (see recipes below). Heat one 10½-ounce can chicken vegetable soup according to label directions; keep warm until ready to serve.

Warm Cherry Pudding

one 16-ounce can sour
cherries, drained
1 cup brown sugar, firmly
packed
½ teaspoon cinnamon
½ cup granulated sugar
3 tablespoons butter or
margarine, softened
1 cup all-purpose flour
1 teaspoon baking powder
½ cup milk
½ cup boiling water
ice cream (optional)

1. Preheat oven to 400° F.

2. In small bowl, mix drained cherries, brown sugar and cinnamon; set aside.

3. In medium bowl, cream together granulated sugar and butter or margarine. Add flour, baking powder and milk. Spoon into lightly greased 8 x 8 x 2-inch baking pan.

4. Spoon cherry mixture over batter. Pour boiling water over all. Bake for 30 minutes. Serve warm, with ice cream if desired.

Sausages and Peppers in Pita Pockets

1 **pound sweet Italian-style sausages**

1 **pound hot Italian-style sausages**

4 **cups julienne strips green pepper**

2 **cups onion rings**

½ **teaspoon salt**

½ **teaspoon oregano**

¼ **teaspoon pepper**

1 **package pita pocket bread (8 small breads)**

1. Cut sausages diagonally into 1-inch slices. Place sausage slices in large skillet; cover and sauté over medium heat until golden brown, about 8 to 10 minutes, stirring frequently.

2. Add green pepper strips, onion rings, salt, oregano and pepper to skillet. Reduce heat to low; cover and continue to cook until sausages are cooked through and vegetables are crisp-tender.

3. While filling is cooking, warm pita breads in oven. Split each open at one end and fill with sausages and peppers.

BEANTOWN BAKED DINNER

Grapefruit Halves

Franks, Bacon and Beans

Boston Brown Bread
Carrots with Chives

Warm Fruit over Ice Cream

Serves 4.

WORK PLAN: Divide 1½ pints vanilla ice cream among 4 dessert dishes; freeze. Prepare Franks, Bacon and Beans (see recipe below). Section 4 grapefruit halves; chill. Prepare one 16-ounce polybag frozen baby carrots according to label directions; drain, and toss with ¼ cup snipped fresh or frozen chives. Slice one 16-ounce canned loaf of Boston brown bread; place in plastic bag and microwave on high setting for 1 minute, until hot. At dessert time, prepare Warm Fruit (see recipe below) and spoon over ice cream.

Franks, Bacon and Beans

4 **slices bacon, cut in half**

one **16-ounce can baked beans**

¼ **cup finely chopped onion**

2 **tablespoons ketchup**

1 **tablespoon honey**

1 **tablespoon prepared spicy mustard**

1 **pound frankfurters, cut into ½-inch slices**

1. Place bacon between paper towels on plate; microwave for 2 minutes on high setting.

2. In large bowl, combine beans, onion, ketchup, honey, mustard and sliced frankfurters.

3. Divide mixture among four 10-ounce custard cups or individual casserole dishes. Top each with 2 pieces partially cooked bacon; cover each with waxed paper.

4. Arrange dishes on floor of microwave oven. Microwave on high setting for 8 to 10 minutes, until mixture bubbles. Let stand for 3 minutes at room temperature before serving.

Warm Fruit

one 11-ounce can fruit cocktail, drained

¼ cup flaked coconut

2 tablespoons rum, brandy or other liqueur

1. Place drained fruit cocktail and coconut in 1-quart glass bowl or casserole. Microwave on high setting for 2 minutes.

2. Stir in rum, brandy or other liqueur. Spoon over ice cream.

HOCKEY PLAYERS' MEAL

Broiled Kielbasa with Mustard Dressing

Hot Rye Bread
Sauerkraut

Apple Pancakes with Cinnamon Sugar

Serves 4.

WORK PLAN: Heat one 16-ounce can or package sauerkraut according to label directions; keep warm. Make dessert by preparing packaged pancake mix for 4 servings, adding 1 cup grated apple and cooking according to label directions. Keep pancakes warm; serve sprinkled with cinnamon sugar. Slice rye loaf; reassemble, wrap in foil and warm in oven while making Kielbasa with Mustard Dressing (see recipe below). Remove rye bread from oven and keep warm while broiling the kielbasa.

Broiled Kielbasa with Mustard Dressing

2-pound kielbasa ring

¼ cup dry unseasoned bread crumbs

2 tablespoons chopped parsley

2 tablespoons prepared mild mustard

1 tablespoon grated Parmesan cheese

1 tablespoon white wine or water

1. Preheat broiler.

2. Cut kielbasa into 4 sections; split each section down center and open, butterfly-fashion.

3. In small bowl, mix bread crumbs, parsley, mustard, grated cheese and wine or water.

4. Arrange kielbasa cut side down in baking pan. Broil 4 inches from heat until browned. Turn cut side up and spread one-fourth of mustard dressing over each kielbasa section. Broil until dressing is brown and bubbling, about 4 minutes.

**SUPPER FOR
THE LATE SHOW**

Fruit Cup

**Sweet Potato Sauté,
Scrapple and Eggs**

Buttery Kale

Pound Cake with Hot
Vanilla Sauce

Serves 4.

WORK PLAN: Prepare appetizer by dividing one 20-ounce can fruit cocktail among 4 serving dishes; chill. Cook two 10-ounce packages frozen kale according to label directions; drain, then toss with 2 tablespoons butter or margarine. Keep kale warm while preparing Sweet Potato Sauté, Scrapple and Eggs (see recipe below). For dessert, prepare vanilla sauce by heating two 5-ounce individual-size cans vanilla pudding with ½ cup heavy cream; serve with slices of pound cake.

Sweet Potato Sauté, Scrapple and Eggs

1½ **pounds sweet potatoes**

½ **cup butter or margarine**

3 **tablespoons brown sugar**

¼ **teaspoon cinnamon**

⅛ **teaspoon ginger**

⅛ **teaspoon nutmeg**

½ **pound scrapple, cut into
4 slices**

4 **eggs**

¼ **cup chopped parsley**

1. Peel potatoes and slice thinly. Melt ¼ cup of the butter or margarine in large skillet over medium heat; add potatoes and sauté until tender and brown, about 10 minutes, turning frequently.

2. Sprinkle potatoes with brown sugar, cinnamon, ginger and nutmeg. Cover and heat just until sugar is melted. Remove potatoes to heated serving platter; keep warm.

3. Melt remaining butter or margarine in another skillet over medium heat; add scrapple slices and fry until brown and crispy, turning frequently. Place on top of sweet potatoes.

4. Fry the eggs in scrapple drippings in skillet; place 1 egg on each slice of scrapple. Sprinkle with parsley.

**DINNER FOR
NEW YEAR'S EVE**

Pâté with Crackers

**Grilled Parslied Lamb
Chops**

Duchess Potatoes
Zucchini and Pea Casserole

Grapes with Brie Cheese

Serves 4.

WORK PLAN: Cut pâté from one 8-ounce can into thin slices. Arrange on 4 lettuce-lined salad plates along with crisp bread and tiny cornichons (gherkins); chill. Make instant mashed potatoes to yield 4 servings. Place potatoes in 8 mounds on greased cookie sheet. Brush with beaten egg and bake at 400° F for 10 minutes or until golden brown; keep warm. Melt 2 tablespoons butter or margarine in large skillet over medium heat; add 2 cups julienne strips zucchini and one 10-ounce package frozen peas and cook until tender. Sprinkle in 1 teaspoon salt and ½ teaspoon nutmeg. Prepare Grilled Parslied Lamb Chops (see recipe below). For dessert, arrange chilled bunches of red, green and purple grapes on 4 dessert plates; add a wedge of Brie cheese, at room temperature, to each. *Shown on page 72.*

Grilled Parslied Lamb Chops

4 lamb loin chops, ¾ to
1 inch thick

3 tablespoons olive oil

1 clove garlic, crushed

½ cup dry unseasoned
bread crumbs

¼ cup chopped parsley

½ teaspoon salt

¼ teaspoon pepper

1. Preheat broiler.

2. Wipe lamb chops with damp paper towels and brush lightly with a little of mixture of oil and crushed garlic. Broil 4 inches from heat, 4 to 7 minutes per side.

3. In small bowl, blend bread crumbs, parsley, salt and pepper. Stir in remaining oil-garlic mixture.

4. Divide crumb mixture among lamb chops, pressing to coat one side only. Broil until topping is crisp and brown, about 1 minute.

**SOMETHING
FROM SUNNY ITALY**

Chicken Cacciatore

Spaghetti
Relishes

Ricotta Parfaits
Serves 4.

WORK PLAN: Prepare Chicken Cacciatore (see recipe below). Prepare dessert by combining one 16-ounce container ricotta or small curd cottage cheese, ½ cup milk-chocolate-flavored cocoa mix, ½ cup finely chopped mixed candied fruits, ½ cup chopped walnuts and 2 teaspoons instant coffee. Divide among 4 parfait glasses; chill. Prepare relishes of cucumber and zucchini sticks, whole radishes and black and green olives; chill on serving tray. Cook one 16-ounce package spaghetti according to label directions.

Chicken Cacciatore

2½- to 3-pound broiler-
fryer chicken, cut into
serving pieces

¼ cup flour

¼ cup vegetable oil

¼ cup chopped onion

1 clove garlic, crushed

one 14½-ounce can stewed
tomatoes

one 4-ounce can mushroom
pieces

¼ cup dry white wine

1 chicken bouillon cube

½ teaspoon thyme

1. Wash chicken pieces under cold running water; pat dry with paper towels. Sprinkle chicken with flour, rubbing into all surfaces.

2. Heat oil in large heavy saucepan over medium heat; add chicken pieces and sauté for about 10 minutes, turning to brown all sides. Add onion and garlic; stir well and cook 3 minutes longer. Add tomatoes, undrained mushroom pieces, wine, bouillon cube and thyme. Reduce heat to low and simmer, covered, for 30 minutes or until chicken is tender.

**SPICY
WARM-ME-UP
MENU**

Indian Chicken Motia

Curried Potatoes and Peas

**Halawapetha Squash
Pudding**

Serves 4.

WORK PLAN: Prepare Indian Chicken Motia (see recipe below). While it simmers, cook 2 cups diced peeled potatoes in boiling salted water; drain. In separate pan, cook two 10-ounce packages frozen peas according to label directions; drain and combine with potatoes. Melt ¼ cup butter or margarine in medium saucepan over medium heat; add 2 teaspoons curry and sauté for 2 minutes. Stir in 2 tablespoons lemon juice; stir in vegetables and heat over low heat for about 5 minutes, stirring occasionally. Make Halawapetha Squash Pudding (see recipe below).

Indian Chicken Motia

2½- to 3-pound broiler-
  fryer chicken, cut into
  serving pieces
1 teaspoon ginger
½ teaspoon pepper
2 tablespoons vegetable oil
one 16-ounce container
  unflavored yogurt
¼ cup finely chopped
  onion
1 tablespoon chili powder
1 teaspoon salt

1. Wash chicken well under cold running water; pat dry with paper towels. Sprinkle chicken pieces with ginger and pepper.

2. Heat oil in large skillet over medium heat; add chicken and sauté for about 5 minutes, turning to brown all sides.

3. Reduce heat to low; stir in yogurt, onion, chili powder and salt. Turn chicken to coat well in sauce. Cook, covered, for 25 to 30 minutes or until chicken is tender, turning frequently.

Halawapetha Squash Pudding

2 tablespoons butter or
  margarine
one 10- to 12-ounce package
  frozen squash
¼ cup brown sugar, firmly
  packed
¼ cup milk
¼ cup chopped almonds
½ teaspoon nutmeg
½ teaspoon cardamom
  (optional)

1. Melt butter or margarine in medium saucepan over low heat; add squash and cook for about 10 minutes, stirring to break into small pieces.

2. Beat in brown sugar, milk, almonds, nutmeg, and cardamom if desired. Cook until well blended and very hot, stirring constantly. Divide among 4 individual dessert dishes; serve warm.

FABULOUS FUSSLESS FEAST

Cucumber Salad

Paprika Chicken with Onion Sauce

Wide Noodles
Baby Beets

Nut Torte

Serves 4.

WORK PLAN: Prepare dessert: With steel all-purpose blade in place in food processor, chop 1 cup whole walnuts. Cut two 9-inch store-bought layer cakes horizontally in half to form 4 layers. Assemble torte, spreading 2 tablespoons raspberry preserves and 2 tablespoons of the chopped nuts over each layer; frost top and sides of cake with some chocolate frosting from one 16-ounce can and sprinkle with remaining nuts. Next, prepare Paprika Chicken with Onion Sauce (see recipe below). Prepare one 16-ounce package wide egg noodles according to label directions. Heat two 16-ounce cans whole baby beets according to label directions; keep warm. With steel slicing blade in place in food processor, thinly slice 3 pared cucumbers, pressing through tube in food processor lid. Blend with ¾ cup sour cream, ¼ cup lemon juice and ¼ teaspoon pepper; divide among 4 lettuce-lined salad plates.

Paprika Chicken with Onion Sauce

2½- to 3-pound broiler-fryer chicken, cut into serving pieces

3 tablespoons butter or margarine

2 tablespoons vegetable oil

1 tablespoon flour

½ cup milk

½ cup chicken broth

1 medium onion, peeled and quartered

½ teaspoon salt

¼ teaspoon pepper

2 tablespoons mild paprika

1. Wash chicken pieces well under cold running water; pat dry with paper towels. Heat 2 tablespoons of the butter or margarine and the oil in large skillet over medium heat; add chicken and sauté for about 10 minutes, turning to brown all sides. Reduce heat to low and cook, covered, for 30 minutes or until chicken is tender, turning chicken twice.

2. Melt remaining 1 tablespoon butter or margarine in small saucepan over low heat; stir in flour and cook for 1 minute. With steel all-purpose blade in place in food processor, place butter-flour mixture in food processor bowl. Slowly pour milk and chicken broth through tube in processor lid, processing as the liquid is poured.

3. Add onion, salt and pepper to processor bowl. Finely chop onion by rapidly turning machine on and off for 10 seconds. Pour mixture into saucepan; simmer for about 10 minutes, until thickened.

4. Place chicken on serving platter; pour all but 2 tablespoons drippings from skillet. Stir paprika into drippings in skillet; pour over chicken. Serve sauce alongside.

Company Walnut Chicken

Poppy Seed Noodles
Pungent Green Beans

Spiced Peach Halves

Serves 4.

WORK PLAN: Prepare Company Walnut Chicken (see recipe below). Make dessert by draining one 20-ounce can cling peach halves and placing peaches cut side up in lightly greased 8 x 8 x 2-inch baking dish. Sprinkle with mixture of ¼ cup brown sugar and ½ teaspoon each cinnamon and ginger. Bake at 350° F for 20 minutes. Serve with 1 cup heavy cream, stiffly beaten and flavored with ½ teaspoon almond extract. Cook two 10-ounce packages frozen green beans according to label directions; drain, and stir in 2 tablespoons butter or margarine and 2 tablespoons wine vinegar. Cook one 16-ounce package egg noodles according to label directions; drain, then toss with ¼ cup sour cream and 2 tablespoons poppy seeds.

Company Walnut Chicken

2½- to 3-pound broiler-fryer chicken, cut into serving pieces

2 tablespoons flour

1 teaspoon salt

¼ teaspoon pepper

2 tablespoons vegetable oil

¼ cup finely chopped green onion

1 cup chicken broth

1 teaspoon rosemary, crumbled

1 teaspoon grated lemon rind

1 cup sour cream

¼ cup chopped walnuts

1. Wash chicken under cold running water; pat dry with paper towels. Sprinkle all surfaces of chicken with flour, salt and pepper.

2. Heat oil in large skillet over medium heat; sauté chicken pieces for about 10 minutes, turning to brown all sides. Add green onion; sauté 3 minutes longer.

3. Add chicken broth, rosemary and lemon rind. Reduce heat to low and simmer, covered, for 25 minutes or until chicken is tender. Remove chicken to heated serving platter; keep warm.

4. Using wire whisk, beat sour cream into drippings in skillet; stir in walnuts. Heat until very hot but do not boil. Pour over chicken.

TimeSaving Tip: Pasta is a staple that all busy cooks should have at the ready. Few pastas take longer than 10 minutes to cook, and many are ready in less than 5 minutes. Look for quick-cooking fettuccine, linguine and spaghettini, and flavorful spinach noodles and hearty whole-wheat spaghetti. Experiment with interesting shapes like butterflies, corkscrews and cartwheels. Cook all pasta until barely tender, or *al dente*, drain it and serve it at once.

**CANTONESE DINNER
DELUXE**

Egg Drop Soup

**Chinese Chicken and
Cashews**

Hot Noodles and Bean
Sprouts

Lemon-Orange Parfaits with
Pineapple Sauce

Serves 4.

WORK PLAN: To make dessert, alternately layer 1½ pints lemon sherbet with mandarin orange slices from one 11-ounce can in 4 large parfait glasses; top each with a little crushed pineapple from one 8-ounce can and freeze. Prepare soup by heating two 10¾-ounce cans chicken bouillon according to label directions; drizzle 2 beaten eggs into boiling bouillon to form thin "noodles"; keep soup warm. Prepare Chinese Chicken and Cashews (see recipe below). Cook one 8-ounce package egg noodles according to label directions; drain, then toss with one 16-ounce can bean sprouts, drained. Heat mixture over very low heat for 2 minutes.

Chinese Chicken and Cashews

**4 chicken breast halves,
skinned and boned**

**2 tablespoons butter or
margarine**

**one 1½-ounce package
onion soup mix**

1 cup water

**one 10-ounce package
frozen Chinese-style
vegetables**

1 cup salted cashews

1 tablespoon dry sherry

¼ teaspoon ginger

1. Wash chicken breast halves under cold running water; pat dry with paper towels. Cut chicken into ¾-inch cubes.

2. Melt butter or margarine in large skillet over medium heat; add chicken cubes and sauté for about 5 minutes, turning to brown all sides.

3. Add onion soup mix and water; stir well. Reduce heat to low and simmer, covered, for 5 minutes. Add frozen vegetables, cashews, sherry and ginger. Continue cooking until vegetables are crisp-tender, about 2 to 3 minutes, stirring constantly.

Ⓧ *TimeSaving Tip:* An instant fillip for any fast menu is a measure of good wine. Two or three flavorful domestic wines should be basic to your kitchen supplies. Have a dry to medium-dry sherry, a dry white wine and a full-bodied red wine on hand. Avoid specially seasoned "cooking" wines as well as sweet wines (though the latter can be used in some desserts). Never cook with a wine you wouldn't drink; in fact, a splash of wine from the bottle you intend to serve with dinner will often complement the main dish perfectly.

MEXICAN MEAL IN MINUTES

Hearty Vegetable Soup

Chicken Tostados

Refried Beans

Mexican Pudding

Serves 4.

WORK PLAN: Prepare dessert by blending three 5-ounce individual-size cans chocolate pudding with 2 tablespoons coffee liqueur or 2 teaspoons instant coffee; fold in 1 cup heavy cream, stiffly beaten. Spoon mixture into large dessert bowl; sprinkle with ¼ cup chopped almonds and chill. Melt 2 tablespoons butter or margarine in large skillet over low heat; add two 16-ounce cans refried beans and stir in 2 cloves garlic, crushed. Heat through and keep warm. Make Chicken Tostados (see recipe below). To make soup, heat one 10½-ounce can minestrone with one 10½-ounce can beef broth, one 16-ounce can chick peas and ½ cup chopped parsley.

Chicken Tostados

one 5-ounce package tostados

2 tablespoons butter or margarine

½ cup chopped onion

two 6¾-ounce cans chicken chunks

1 tablespoon chili powder

¼ teaspoon oregano

¼ teaspoon cumin

one 8-ounce can Spanish-style tomato sauce

3 to 4 drops hot pepper sauce

½ cup grated mozzarella cheese

½ cup finely shredded lettuce

½ cup chopped tomato

½ cup sour cream

1. Wrap tostados in foil; place in 325° F oven to heat.

2. Melt butter or margarine in medium skillet over medium heat; add onion and sauté until tender, about 5 minutes, stirring constantly. Add chicken; using fork, break into small chunks.

3. Stir in chili powder, oregano and cumin. Blend in ½ cup of the tomato sauce. Reduce heat to low and simmer, covered, for about 10 minutes.

4. While chicken cooks, mix remaining tomato sauce with hot pepper sauce in small bowl. Place grated cheese, shredded lettuce, chopped tomato and sour cream in individual small bowls.

5. To serve, spread 2 tablespoons hot chicken mixture on top of each warm tostado. Top each tostado with hot sauce, cheese, lettuce, tomato and sour cream.

**SIMPLY ELEGANT
CHRISTMAS DINNER**

Hot Buttered Tomato Juice

**Rock Cornish Game Hens
with Apricot Glaze**

Raisin Stuffing
Asparagus Mignonette

Fruit and Cheese Platter

Serves 4.

WORK PLAN: Prepare Rock Cornish Game Hens with Apricot Glaze (see recipe below). Make side dish of stuffing by preparing 2 cups packaged herb stuffing mix according to label directions, adding ½ cup chopped golden raisins. Place stuffing mixture in lightly greased 8 x 8 x 2-inch baking dish and cover dish with foil; bake beside game hens. Cook two 10-ounce packages frozen asparagus spears according to label directions; keep warm, and toss with ¼ cup melted butter or margarine and 1 teaspoon each grated lemon rind and coarsely ground black pepper just before serving. Heat 3 cups spicy tomato juice; divide among 4 mugs and serve with small pat of butter on top of each portion. Arrange fruit and cheese platter to include at least two kinds of cheese—one sharp, one mild and soft. Let stand at room temperature for 30 minutes before serving for dessert.

Rock Cornish Hens with Apricot Glaze

two 1-pound Cornish game
hens, split in half

¼ cup butter or margarine

¼ cup chopped onion

2 cups packaged herb
stuffing mix

½ cup golden raisins

2 tablespoons chopped
parsley

1 egg, beaten

⅔ cup warm water

¼ cup apricot preserves

2 tablespoons orange juice

1. Wash Cornish game hen halves under cold running water; pat dry with paper towels. Set game hens aside.

2. Melt butter or margarine in large skillet over medium heat; add onion and sauté until tender, about 3 minutes. Remove from heat. Using fork, stir in stuffing mix, golden raisins, parsley, beaten egg and warm water.

3. Stuff each game hen half with one-fourth of stuffing mixture, pressing lightly to adhere to cavity. Place hens stuffing side down in well-greased, large baking pan.

4. Melt apricot preserves with orange juice in small saucepan over medium heat. Brush over game hens. Roast at 475° F for 25 to 30 minutes or until game hens are crisp and tender.

◎ *TimeSaving Tip:* Fruit and cheese provide an immediate happy ending to any meal. Apples, pears and grapes are the best winter fruit buys. Try Cheddar with apples, blue cheese with pears and soft ripe Brie or Camembert with grapes. Dried fruits are delicious with cheese—Swiss and dried dates, soft pepper cheese and figs, and Bel Paese or Port Salut with dried apricots beautifully top off winter dinners.

FAST FOOD
FOR A FREEZING DAY

Marinated Mushrooms

Turkey Mozzarella

Hot Crusty Bread
Watercress-Chicory Salad

Tortoni

Serves 4.

WORK PLAN: Divide two 8-ounce cans button mushrooms, drained, among 4 lettuce-lined salad plates; pour 2 tablespoons garlic salad dressing over each and chill. Make Turkey Mozzarella (see recipe below). In large salad bowl, toss together 2 cups watercress sprigs and 2 cups chicory sprigs; toss with ¼ cup Italian-style salad dressing just before serving. Wrap a loaf of crusty Italian or French bread in foil; heat along with Turkey Mozzarella. To prepare dessert, divide 1½ pints vanilla ice cream among 4 individual dessert dishes; sprinkle each portion with 2 tablespoons each chopped nuts and chopped candied fruits, then freeze.

Turkey Mozzarella

one 16-ounce package sliced turkey breast cutlets

1 egg

1 tablespoon water

1 cup dry seasoned bread crumbs

2 tablespoons butter or margarine

one 15½-ounce jar spaghetti sauce

one 8-ounce package sliced mozzarella or Muenster cheese

1. Separate turkey cutlets. Beat together egg and water; pour onto plate. Place bread crumbs on second plate. Dip cutlets in egg mixture to coat both sides; drain slightly. Dip both sides into bread crumbs; press crumbs firmly to coat.

2. Melt butter or margarine in large skillet over medium heat; add cutlets and sauté to brown, about 2 minutes per side.

3. Spread ¼ cup of the spaghetti sauce over bottom of lightly greased 8 x 8 x 2-inch baking dish. Arrange 4 turkey cutlets over sauce and top with half of cheese slices; pour half of remaining sauce over cutlets. Repeat layers with remaining cutlets, cheese and sauce. Bake at 400° F for 30 minutes or until casserole is bubbly.

QUICK SUPPER
SAUTE

Chicken Livers, Onions and Spinach

Buttered Whole Wheat Toast
Fingers
Chinese Salad

Heavenly Hash

Serves 4.

WORK PLAN: First prepare salad by combining 4 cups bite-size pieces Chinese cabbage and one 16-ounce can bean sprouts, rinsed and drained; chill. Just before serving, toss with dressing of ⅓ cup vegetable oil and 1 tablespoon each soy sauce, sherry and sesame seeds. Next, make dessert: Combine two 5-ounce individual-size cans chocolate pudding with ¼ cup each semisweet chocolate morsels, chopped walnuts, flaked coconut and snipped miniature marshmallows; divide among 4 dessert glasses and chill until serving time. Prepare Chicken Livers, Onions and Spinach (see recipe below); serve with buttered toast fingers.

Chicken Livers, Onions and Spinach

1 **pound chicken livers**
¼ **cup soy sauce**
½ **teaspoon ginger**
¼ **cup flour**
¼ **cup vegetable oil**
2 **cups thin red onion rings**
½ **pound spinach, washed**
  and stems removed

1. Wash chicken livers well under cold running water; pat dry with paper towels. Cut in half with scissors, snipping away and discarding any surplus fat.

2. In medium bowl, blend soy sauce and ginger. Stir in chicken livers to coat well; marinate at room temperature for 15 minutes. Remove chicken livers from marinade; toss with flour to coat well.

3. Heat 2 tablespoons of the oil in large skillet over medium heat; add onion rings and sauté for 2 minutes, stirring constantly. Push to outer edge of pan.

4. Add remaining 2 tablespoons oil to skillet; add chicken livers and sauté for 2 minutes, turning to brown all sides. Add spinach; stir well to combine with chicken livers and onions. Cook just until spinach is slightly wilted.

TimeSaving Tip: Washing and drying salad greens eats up a lot of precious time; so if you often want to serve a last-minute salad with dinner, keep two or three cans of vegetables chilling in the refrigerator. Choose some that have crunch, like bean sprouts, water chestnuts and piquant gherkins; invest in others with texture and eye appeal—whole green beans, red kidney beans, wax beans, firm garbanzos and cannellini. Try different combinations of vegetables, always looking for contrasting textures and compatible tastes. If there's some time to spare, toss in some sliced celery or green pepper. Make sure you have a supply of dressings—bottled or homemade—to quickly toss in with your speedy salad, along with a sprinkling of dried herbs. Saving time doesn't have to mean cutting down on taste!

WINTER FISHERMEN'S MEAL

Tomato Soup

Fish with Herb Stuffing

Chopped Buttered Broccoli
Waldorf Salad

Banana Cream Pie

Serves 4.

WORK PLAN: Prepare Banana Cream Pie (see recipe below). Then prepare salad: Combine 2 cups sliced unpeeled apples, 1 cup sliced celery, ½ cup chopped walnuts, ½ cup mayonnaise and 1 tablespoon Dijon-style mustard; place on platter lined with celery leaves and chill. Prepare Fish with Herb Stuffing (see recipe below). While fish is cooking, place two 10-ounce packages frozen chopped broccoli, broken into small pieces, in medium-size glass bowl, adding water and salt according to label directions; cover bowl with plastic wrap. Mix one 10¾-ounce can tomato soup according to label directions; divide among 4 soup mugs. Microwave vegetable and soup on high setting; remove soup after 1 minute and microwave broccoli 3 minutes longer.

Banana Cream Pie

one 9-inch frozen prepared
pie shell

1 tablespoon vanilla extract

one 3¾-ounce package
banana pudding and pie
filling

2 cups milk

2 bananas

2 tablespoons lemon juice

1 cup heavy cream

1. Transfer frozen pie shell from metal to glass pie plate. Using pastry brush, paint edge of pastry shell with vanilla extract to give browned appearance. Prick bottom and sides of crust with fork.

2. Microwave crust on high setting for 6 to 7 minutes, rotating a half turn in middle of cooking time. Cool slightly.

3. In 4-cup glass measure, blend banana pudding and pie filling and milk, mixing very well. Microwave on high setting for 6 minutes; stir twice during last 2 minutes of cooking time.

4. Slice bananas; toss with lemon juice. Pour half of pudding mixture into pie shell; top with half of bananas and pour remaining pudding mixture over banana layer. Freeze until serving time.

5. Just before serving, use electric mixer at high speed to beat cream in small bowl until stiff peaks form. Spread over pie; decorate around edge with remaining banana slices.

Fish with Herb Stuffing

¼ cup water

½ cup butter or margarine

¾ cup packaged herb stuffing mix

¼ cup chopped onion

1½ pounds fish fillets (whiting, flounder, sole or cod)

paprika

lemon slices

1. Combine water and ¼ cup of the butter or margarine in medium-size glass bowl. Microwave on high setting for 2 minutes, until butter or margarine is melted. Stir in stuffing mix; set aside.

2. Place 2 tablespoons of the remaining butter or margarine and the chopped onion on nonmetal serving platter. Cover platter with waxed paper; microwave on high setting for 2 minutes. Combine stuffing with onion on serving platter.

3. Wipe fish fillets with damp paper towels; arrange fish over stuffing. Dot with remaining 2 tablespoons butter or margarine; sprinkle lightly with paprika. Arrange lemon slices down center of fish.

4. Cover platter with plastic wrap; microwave on high setting for 7 to 8 minutes or until fish flakes easily when tested with a fork. Let stand at room temperature for 2 minutes before serving.

MORE TUNA MAGIC

Tuna Casserole

Mixed Vegetable Sauté

Chocolate Bit Brownies

Serves 4.

WORK PLAN: Prepare Chocolate Bit Brownies, then Tuna Casserole (see recipes below). While the casserole is cooking, combine one 10-ounce package frozen peas and carrots and one 10-ounce package frozen corn kernels in medium-size glass bowl, breaking vegetables into small pieces. Add ½ cup water, 2 tablespoons butter or margarine, 1½ teaspoons salt and ¼ teaspoon pepper. Cover bowl with plastic wrap; microwave on high setting for 4 to 5 minutes while Tuna Casserole is standing at room temperature.

Chocolate Bit Brownies

⅓ cup butter or margarine

four 1-ounce squares unsweetened chocolate

1 cup sugar

2 eggs, beaten

1 cup all-purpose flour

½ teaspoon baking powder

one 6-ounce package semisweet chocolate morsels

Makes 16.

1. Place butter or margarine and chocolate in medium-size glass mixing bowl. Microwave on high setting for 1½ to 2 minutes or until chocolate is melted.

2. Stir in sugar; add beaten eggs and beat well. Blend in flour, baking powder and chocolate morsels. Spoon mixture into ungreased 8 x 8 x 2-inch baking pan.

3. Microwave on 50% power for 7 minutes, rotating pan a half turn in middle of cooking time; microwave on high setting 3 to 4 minutes longer, until brownies are dry on top. Place pan on wire rack to cool. Cut brownies into 2-inch squares.

Tuna Casserole

one 10¾-ounce can cream of mushroom soup

1 cup water

two 7-ounce cans tuna, drained and flaked

one 6-ounce can water chestnuts, drained and sliced

one 4-ounce can sliced mushrooms, drained

one 3-ounce can French-fried onion rings

one 16-ounce can crisp chow mein noodles

1. Combine soup and water in 2-quart glass casserole. Stir in drained, flaked tuna, sliced water chestnuts, drained mushrooms, onion rings and 1 cup of the chow mein noodles.

2. Cover casserole with glass lid or plastic wrap. Microwave on high setting for 6 minutes, rotating casserole a half turn in middle of cooking time.

3. Let stand, covered, at room temperature for 5 minutes. Sprinkle with remaining noodles.

EASY-DOES-IT DINNER

Eggs Oriental

Peas and Carrots
Buttered Rice

Chinese Salad with Ginger Dressing

Pineapple and Lychees
Fortune Cookies

Serves 4.

WORK PLAN: Prepare salad by tossing together 2 cups shredded Chinese cabbage, one 10-ounce package snow peas, thawed (do this quickly by placing snow peas under running water and patting dry), and one 5-ounce can bamboo shoots, drained; place in 4 individual serving bowls and top with dressing of ½ cup each mayonnaise and sour cream and 1 teaspoon ginger. Prepare dessert by combining one 16-ounce can each pineapple chunks and lychees in large dessert bowl; chill, and serve with fortune cookies. Cook one 16-ounce polybag frozen peas and carrots according to label directions; keep warm. Prepare 1 cup long-grain rice according to label directions; keep warm. Prepare Eggs Oriental (see recipe below).

Eggs Oriental

2 tablespoons vegetable oil

1 cup canned bean sprouts, rinsed and drained

6 eggs

½ cup finely chopped celery

½ cup finely chopped mushrooms

¼ cup chopped green onion

½ teaspoon salt

¼ teaspoon pepper

1. Heat oil in large skillet over medium heat; add bean sprouts and sauté for 2 to 3 minutes, stirring occasionally.

2. In medium bowl, beat eggs, celery, mushrooms, green onion, salt and pepper. Pour into skillet and reduce heat to low; using fork, mix well with bean sprouts.

3. Cook eggs until set, with bottom surface lightly browned and top surface moist and shiny. Cut into 4 wedges.

**DINNER
WITH FLAIR**

Mongol Soup

Crusty Deviled Cheese Pie

Peas and Lettuce
Broccoli Spears

Bananas Flambé

Serves 4.

WORK PLAN: Prepare Crusty Deviled Cheese Pie (see recipe below). While pie bakes, prepare soup by blending one 11¼-ounce can green pea soup, one 10¾-ounce can tomato soup and 1½ cups milk; heat and keep warm. Prepare two 10-ounce packages frozen peas according to label directions, adding ½ cup shredded lettuce; keep warm. Prepare one 10-ounce package frozen broccoli spears according to label directions; keep warm. For dessert, prepare Bananas Flambé (see recipe below).

Crusty Deviled Cheese Pie

2 cups grated Swiss cheese

one 4½-ounce can deviled ham

2 eggs

½ cup evaporated milk or half-and-half

2 tablespoons instant minced onion

one 7-inch frozen prepared pie shell

¼ cup dry unseasoned bread crumbs

¼ cup grated Parmesan cheese

1 tablespoon chopped parsley

2 tablespoons butter or margarine, melted

1. Preheat oven to 400° F.

2. In medium bowl, mix together Swiss cheese and deviled ham. Add eggs, evaporated milk or half-and-half and minced onion; beat to blend well. Pour into pie shell.

3. In small bowl, mix together bread crumbs, Parmesan cheese, parsley and melted butter or margarine. Sprinkle over cheese mixture to form top crust. Bake for 30 minutes or until knife inserted in center comes out clean.

Bananas Flambé

4 bananas

¼ cup butter or margarine

¼ cup brown sugar, firmly packed

1 tablespoon lemon juice

¼ cup white rum

ice cream (optional)

1. Peel bananas and cut lengthwise in half. Melt butter or margarine in large skillet over medium heat; add bananas and sauté, 30 seconds per side.

2. Sprinkle with brown sugar and lemon juice; reduce heat to low and simmer, covered, until very hot but still firm.

3. Pour rum over bananas; heat for 1 minute and ignite. Let flame burn down completely. Serve topped with ice cream if desired.

**MARIA'S
MONTEREY
SUPPER**

Spiced Beef Bouillon

Chili con Queso

Pinto Beans
Shredded Lettuce
Sliced Tomatoes

Mocha-Cinnamon Desserts

Serves 4.

WORK PLAN: Prepare desserts by gently blending two 5-ounce individual-size cans chocolate pudding, 1 cup refrigerator dessert topping, 2 teaspoons instant coffee and ½ teaspoon cinnamon; divide among 4 parfait glasses and chill. Prepare 3 cups shredded lettuce and slice 4 tomatoes; chill. Heat two 15-ounce cans pinto beans in chili sauce according to label directions. Prepare Chili con Queso (see recipe below). Heat one 10½-ounce can beef bouillon according to label directions, adding 3 to 4 drops hot pepper sauce.

Chili con Queso

one 16-ounce can tortillas

TOPPING

2 tablespoons butter or margarine

¼ cup chopped onion

one 8-ounce can tomato sauce

one 4-ounce can taco sauce

½ teaspoon salt

¼ teaspoon pepper

2 cups diced mild Cheddar cheese

one 3½-ounce can mild or hot chilies, drained

1 cup evaporated milk or half-and-half

1. Place tortillas on baking sheet between two clean damp cloths. Heat in 325° F oven while preparing topping.

2. To prepare topping, melt butter or margarine in medium saucepan over medium heat; add onion and sauté until tender, about 3 minutes. Add tomato sauce, taco sauce, salt and pepper; reduce heat to low and simmer, covered, for 5 minutes.

3. Add diced cheese and drained chilies; stir until cheese is melted. Add evaporated milk or half-and-half; heat 2 minutes longer. Serve over hot tortillas.

FAMILY SANDWICH SUPPER

Celery and Radishes
Onion-Anchovy Dip

Muenster Loaf Supreme

Baked Mushrooms
French-Fried Onion Rings

Apricot-Prune Parfaits

Serves 4.

WORK PLAN: Start by making Apricot-Prune Parfaits (see recipe below). Next, prepare appetizer: Wash 4 stalks celery and cut into 3-inch strips; wash 1 package of radishes and cut them lengthwise in half. Chill celery and radishes. Make dip by mixing one ¾-ounce package onion soup mix, 1 tablespoon anchovy paste and 1 cup sour cream; chill. Drain two 8-ounce cans mushroom caps and place mushrooms and 2 tablespoons butter or margarine in 1-quart covered casserole; place in oven to heat along with French-fried onion rings from one 16-ounce package. Prepare Muenster Loaf Supreme (see recipe below).

Apricot-Prune Parfaits

1 cup heavy cream

¼ cup confectioners' sugar

½ teaspoon vanilla extract

two 4½-ounce jars baby food pureed apricots

two 4½-ounce jars baby food pureed prunes

1. Using electric mixer at high speed, beat cream in medium bowl until stiff; quickly beat in confectioners' sugar and vanilla extract.

2. Alternately layer whipped cream, apricots and prunes in 4 large dessert glasses, ending with whipped cream.

Muenster Loaf Supreme

1 small loaf Italian or French bread

¼ cup butter or margarine, melted

2 tablespoons chopped parsley

2 tablespoons sesame seeds

4 Muenster cheese slices, halved

4 boiled ham slices, halved

8 slices tomato, ¼ inch thick

1. Cut loaf into 8 slices, cutting to within ¼ inch of bottom. Brush all cut surfaces with melted butter or margarine. Sprinkle with parsley and sesame seeds.

2. Between each slice, place half a cheese slice, half a ham slice and 2 tomato slices. Arrange loaf on sheet of aluminum foil; crumple foil to form a container coming one-third of the way up. Bake at 450° F for 10 to 15 minutes or until ham and tomatoes are hot and cheese is melted and bubbly.

Index